MATT AND TOM OLDFIELD

ULTIMATE FOOTBALL HEROES

LUKAKU

FROM THE PLAYGROUND
TO THE PITCH

DINO

Published by Dino Books
an imprint of John Blake Publishing
3 Bramber Court, 2 Bramber Road,
London W14 9PB, England

www.johnblakepublishing.co.uk

www.facebook.com/johnblakebooks 📘
twitter.com/jblakebooks 📧

This edition published in 2018

ISBN: 978 1 78606 885 9

British Library Cataloguing-in-Publication Data:

A catalogue record for this book is available from the British Library.

Design by www.envydesign.co.uk

Printed and bound in Great Britain by Clays Ltd, St Ives plc

1 3 5 7 9 10 8 6 4 2

Papers used by John Blake Publishing are natural, recyclable products made from
wood grown in sustainable forests. The manufacturing processes conform to the
environmental regulations of the country of origin.

Every attempt has been made to contact the relevant copyright-holders, but some
were unobtainable. We would be grateful if the appropriate people could contact us.

John Blake Publishing is an imprint of Bonnier Publishing.
www.bonnierpublishing.co.uk

For Noah and Nico,
Southampton's future strikeforce

ULTIMATE
FOOTBALL HEROES

Matt Oldfield is an accomplished writer and the editor-in-chief
of football review site *Of Pitch & Page*. Tom Oldfield is a freelance
sports writer and the author of biographies on Cristiano Ronaldo,
Arsène Wenger and Rafael Nadal.

Cover illustration by Dan Leydon.
To learn more about Dan visit danleydon.com
To purchase his artwork visit etsy.com/shop/footynews
Or just follow him on Twitter @danleydon

TABLE OF CONTENTS

ACKNOWLEDGEMENTS 7

CHAPTER 1 – **DEBUT GOAL IN RED** 9

CHAPTER 2 – **BIG BOY** 16

CHAPTER 3 – **'MY FRIEND VINNIE'** 21

CHAPTER 4 – **LIKE FATHER, LIKE SON** 28

CHAPTER 5 – **RUPEL BOOM** 34

CHAPTER 6 – **WINTAM** 40

CHAPTER 7 – **SCOUTED** 46

CHAPTER 8 – **HARD WORK AT ANDERLECHT** 52

CHAPTER 9 – **PURPLE TALENTS** 58

CHAPTER 10 – **DREAM DEBUT?** 64

CHAPTER 11 – **RISING STAR**. 70

CHAPTER 12 – **CHELSEA DREAM PART I**. 77

CHAPTER 13 – **CHELSEA DREAM PART II**. 84

CHAPTER 14 – **SLOW START** 90

CHAPTER 15 – **ROMELU & PAUL** 96

CHAPTER 16 – **WEST BROM**. 101

CHAPTER 17 – **EVERTON PART I** 108

CHAPTER 18 – **BELGIUM**. 117

CHAPTER 19 – **EVERTON PART II** 123

CHAPTER 20 – **ROMELU & ROSS**. 130

CHAPTER 21 – **EURO 2016** 136

CHAPTER 22 – **NEXT LEVEL**. 143

CHAPTER 23 – **THE MOVE TO MANCHESTER** 150

ACKNOWLEDGEMENTS

First of all, I'd like to thank John Blake Publishing – and particularly my editor James Hodgkinson – for giving me the opportunity to work on these books and for supporting me throughout. Writing stories for the next generation of football fans is both an honour and a pleasure.

I wouldn't be doing this if it wasn't for my brother Tom. I owe him so much and I'm very grateful for his belief in me as an author. I feel like Robin setting out on a solo career after a great partnership with Batman. I hope I do him (Tom, not Batman) justice with these new books.

Next up, I want to thank my friends for keeping

me sane during long hours in front of the laptop. Pang, Will, Mills, Doug, John, Charlie – the laughs and the cups of coffee are always appreciated.

I've already thanked my brother but I'm also very grateful to the rest of my family, especially Melissa, Noah and of course Mum and Dad. To my parents, I owe my biggest passions: football and books. They're a real inspiration for everything I do.

Finally, I couldn't have done this without Iona's encouragement and understanding during long, work-filled weekends. Much love to you.

CHAPTER 1

DEBUT GOAL IN RED

Tuesday, 8 August 2017

'You wanted to play in big games,' Paul told Romelu before kick-off in Macedonia. 'Well, they don't get much bigger than this!'

Romelu was about to make his Manchester United debut against the European Champions Real Madrid in the UEFA Super Cup. Paul was right; big games didn't get much bigger than that. Romelu would be playing against world-class players like Cristiano Ronaldo, Gareth Bale and Sergio Ramos. He felt nervous but also very excited.

'I belong at this level,' he kept telling himself. He would need every ounce of his self-belief.

Romelu had played in the Super Cup before, for
Chelsea, four years earlier, but Bayern Munich won
the trophy on that awful night when his penalty
was saved by Manuel Neuer. This time Romelu was
determined to replace that painful memory with
something much happier.

Romelu was a completely different player now.
After four successful seasons with West Brom and
Everton, he was no longer merely a youngster with
great potential. At the age of twenty-four, he was now
an experienced Premier League striker with pace,
power and skill. He could do it all. He had proved that
he could score every kind of goal – tap-ins, headers,
one-on-ones and wondergoals – and lots of them.

But this was now the next level. José Mourinho
had paid £75 million to bring him to Old Trafford.
He had been chosen as the man to replace Zlatan
Ibrahimović, one of the best strikers of all time. As
United's big new Number 9, Romelu needed to get
off to a strong goalscoring start against Real Madrid.

'You ready?' Paul asked as they waited in the
tunnel.

Romelu didn't need to reply. His friend could see the fire in his eyes, and could see that Romelu just wanted to get out on the pitch and start playing.

'Let's win this!' Romelu shouted to United's other big new signing, midfielder Nemanja Matić. They had both joined the club to challenge for big trophies like this.

Romelu was really looking forward to his battle with Sergio Ramos and Raphaël Varane. They were two of the best defenders in the world, but he had the pace and power to cause them lots of problems. Romelu felt fearless. With a giant leap, he won his first header against Varane. The fans cheered.

Real Madrid took the lead, but Manchester United didn't panic. There was plenty of time to equalise. When Ander Herrera tackled Toni Kroos, Romelu sprinted towards the ball like a dog after a bone. He got there first but when he took a touch, the referee blew the whistle. The linesman's flag was up – offside!

'Why didn't you leave it?' Ander complained. 'I was right behind you and I was onside!'

'Sorry, I wasn't thinking,' Romelu apologised. 'I was just so eager to score!'

It was a very embarrassing mistake to make, especially with millions of fans watching on TV around the world. Romelu was playing at the top level now, and he needed to use his brain as well as his brawn.

A few minutes later, Paul floated a great cross towards Romelu in the penalty area. Was this his moment? Ramos was marking him tightly but Romelu was taller, stronger and more determined. In the air, he used his neck muscles to flick the ball towards goal. His dad had taught him well but unfortunately, his header was straight at the keeper.

Nearly! Romelu gave Paul a big thumbs-up. Next time, he would do better. He would score.

'We're still in this game,' United manager Mourinho told his players at half-time. 'Romelu's doing a great job up front but let's get forward and support him!'

Real Madrid shocked United by scoring again early in the second half. It looked like game over, but Romelu wasn't giving up on that debut goal.

Paul headed Ander's cross towards goal. The keeper saved it, and the rebound fell at Romelu's feet. This was an even better chance for him to score! He was inside the six-yard box and it was pretty much an open goal. But on the verge of glory, he got too excited. Before he could stop himself, he had blazed his shot high over the bar.

He couldn't believe it. He stood there in the penalty area, staring up at where the ball had gone. It sounded like the Real Madrid fans were laughing at him. Why had he kicked it so hard? Next to him, Paul punched the air in frustration.

'I *have* to make up for that miss,' Romelu told himself as he jogged back into position.

A few minutes later, Nemanja hit a long-range strike. Again, the keeper saved it, but the ball bounced out. Romelu was the first to react and he got there ahead of Ramos. He wasn't going to mess it up this time. He stayed calm and aimed for the bottom corner.

Goooooooooooooooooooooaaaaaaaaaaaaaaaallllllllll llllllllllllllllll!!!!!!!!!!!!!!!!!!

Romelu didn't celebrate; there wasn't time. He grabbed the ball out of the back of the net and ran back for the restart. United still had half an hour to score an equaliser.

'Come on!' Romelu shouted, waving his fist. He was really pumped up now.

Despite his best efforts, though, the match finished 2–1 to Real Madrid. Romelu didn't collect the winner's medal that he wanted, but he did have a debut goal in red.

'Well played,' Mourinho said, patting him on the back. 'You didn't let that miss get to you. You kept going and you got your reward. Congratulations!'

'Thanks, boss,' Romelu replied.

It was great to have his manager's full support. Years before at Chelsea, Mourinho hadn't trusted him in the team. In fact, he sold Romelu to Everton, but that was all forgiven. The disappointment had only made him stronger. Romelu was now a different striker with different teammates, at a different club.

'Do you think they'll stop saying that you don't

score in big games now?' his best friend Vinnie
texted later that night.

Romelu sent a one-word reply – 'No'.

'Really?! But you just scored against Real Madrid!'

Romelu was used to people doubting his
footballing ability. It had been happening for his
whole life, ever since his days as a very tall six-year-
old. Fortunately, he always had his family, friends
and coaches to support him, and he let his goals do
the talking. Yes, he was big and strong, but he was a
lot more than that. He was also talented, professional
and hard-working.

He had proved everyone wrong. Wintam's
wonderkid was now Manchester United's star striker.
Not bad for a big boy from Belgium.

CHAPTER 2

BIG BOY

As she finished the washing-up, Adolphine felt
something tugging at her dress. Had she caught it
on the cupboard door? No, it was actually some*one*
tugging at her dress.

'No Romelu, you can't still be hungry,' she told her
son. His appetite was amazing. 'You just had a big
lunch!'

But her son nodded his head again and again. He
was still hungry! Romelu patted his belly and looked
up with large, pleading eyes. That always made it
hard for his mum to say no. 'Okay fine, you can have
one more slice of bread but then you'll have to wait
until dinner time. Yes?'

Romelu nodded eagerly, took the slice and

crammed it straight into his mouth. After swallowing it down, he went back to playing. Watching this performance, Adolphine rolled her eyes and laughed. 'That boy is incredible!'

'He's growing up fast, just like his dad!' Roger replied proudly.

'Yes, but he's not even three years old yet – how much food will he need when he's a teenager? Unfortunately, money doesn't grow on trees!'

The Lukakus had their own council house – Number 71, Duiventilstraat – in Wintam, a quiet, comfortable village in the north of Belgium. It was a safe environment for bringing up kids but paying for it wasn't easy. Romelu's younger brother, Jordan, would soon be eating like a big boy too. Adolphine worked as a cleaner to help feed her hungry family but it wasn't always enough.

Her husband smiled. 'I'll just need to score more goals then!'

Roger was a striker at the local football club, Rupel Boom. He had left the Democratic Republic of Congo at the age of twenty-three to play in Belgium. It had been a difficult decision for him to leave Africa but there were better job opportunities in Europe. He was doing well at Boom, but the wages were low in the Second Division.

Roger went over to his wife and gave her a comforting hug. 'Remember, we're giving Romelu and Jordan chances that we never had when we were younger. With a good education, they'll get good jobs. Who knows, maybe one of them will be a doctor or a lawyer!'

'Or a footballer,' Adolphine replied as she watched her son.

The footballing dream had all started for Romelu when Roger gave him a mini-football. He thought it would be abandoned after a few minutes, like most of his son's other toys. But instead, it had become Romelu's best friend. He wouldn't go anywhere without it. Sometimes he held it, sometimes he kicked it, sometimes he even used it as a little pillow, but the ball was always there with him.

'Romelu, no!' his mum shouted out as he giggled and threw the ball up into the air. Adolphine caught it before it landed in the kitchen sink. 'How many times have I told you? You can't do that inside!'

Roger grabbed their coats off the hook. 'Come on, son, I think we need to get some fresh air,' he said with a smile.

Romelu loved being outside. As soon as the front door opened, his little face lit up. They were going on an adventure! Holding his dad's hand, he crossed one street and then another. Romelu knew where they were going. As they got closer to their destination, he started to walk faster and faster, dragging Roger along.

It wasn't much to look at. It wasn't a playground with swings and a roundabout. There weren't any football goals or picnic benches. It wasn't very big either, but there was grass and there were trees. Most importantly, there weren't many cars, or other people around. With Roger watching him, Romelu was safe to play. After a few minutes of running, he turned back to his dad.

'What?' Roger asked, shrugging his shoulders dramatically.

Romelu stretched up his hands and stamped his feet impatiently. Roger knew exactly what his son wanted. Waving his arms around like a magician, he pulled out the favourite mini-football.

'Yay!' Romelu clapped and kicked his legs.

He didn't know it yet, but that patch of green would be the start of his great football career.

CHAPTER 3

"MY FRIEND VINNIE"

'So, how was it?' Adolphine asked Romelu as they walked home together after his first day at Huveneers Primary School.

'We played lots of football!' her son said happily, kicking every stone in his path.

'Yes, I noticed,' Adolphine muttered, looking down at the scuffed knees of his new school trousers. She tried again. 'Did you learn lots of new things at school?'

Romelu nodded eagerly. 'I learnt lots of new football tricks!'

Adolphine sighed and blamed her husband. There was no stopping their son's love of football.

As soon as they got through the front door, Romelu rushed off to his bedroom.

'Slow down, what's going on?' his mum asked, looking confused. 'Don't you want a snack?'

There was no answer. A few minutes later, Romelu walked into the kitchen. His school uniform was gone.

'Why are you dressed like that?' Adolphine asked. Her son was wearing full football kit – shirt, shorts, socks and boots.

At that moment, there was a knock at the door. Romelu jumped up out of his chair to go and answer it.

'Hi, Rom!'

'Hi, Vinnie!'

Vinnie had a football under his arm. 'Let's go and play!'

Romelu turned around and called into the kitchen. 'Mum, can I go and play football for a bit?'

Adolphine came to the door. She recognised the small boy with brown hair – he was one of their neighbours.

'Mum, this is my friend Vinnie. He lives up the road and he goes to school with me.'

'Nice to meet you, Vinnie,' Adolphine said with a friendly smile. 'Where are you going to play? You're not old enough to go far, and dinner will be ready soon.'

'We'll just go to the field across the road, Mrs Lukaku,' Vinnie explained politely. 'Rom will be back in an hour, I promise.'

'Please, Mum! Please, please, please!' Romelu begged.

Adolphine nodded slowly. 'Okay, but if you're not back in an hour, there will be BIG trouble.'

'Thanks, Mum!' Romelu shouted behind him as they ran off.

'Be careful when crossing the roads!' Adolphine called out but they were too far away to hear.

Romelu and Vinnie put their jumpers down on the grass. They now had everything they needed – one football and two goalposts.

'I'll shoot first,' Vinnie decided. 'When I score five goals, we'll switch.'

Romelu agreed; it was Vinnie's ball, after all.

Romelu threw himself across the grass to save the first couple of shots. He was already very tall for his age and he was athletic too. He had the skills to be a good goalkeeper but that didn't interest him; he wanted to be a great striker like his dad.

'Goooooaaaaaallllllll!' Vinnie cheered.

Romelu tried to look disappointed but really, he had let the ball go past him on purpose. He was bored of being the keeper. After four more goals, it was finally his turn to shoot.

He dribbled forward as fast as he could. The ball was a long way ahead of him but that didn't matter. There weren't any defenders around to tackle him. As he got near to Vinnie, he pulled back his left foot and kicked it as hard as he could. The ball flew through the air but a long way wide of the goal.

'Wow, that was wild!' Vinnie laughed as he chased after it.

Romelu still had a lot of work to do on his technique but that was okay. He had plenty of time and now he had a friend to practise with. His next shot went in but the one after that sailed wide again. That pattern carried on.

'When you get it on target, it's a goal every time!' Vinnie told him.

That was the big challenge. 'Right, one more shot and then I really have to go home,' Romelu said. He didn't want to make his mum angry.

This time, he didn't sprint, and he didn't blast the ball either. Instead, he looked up and picked his spot carefully. His shot didn't go exactly where he wanted it to go but it was on target and it was too powerful for Vinnie to save.

'Nice one!' his new friend cheered. 'Shall we play again tomorrow?'

Romelu nodded. From that moment onwards, they played football every day. Soon, they were playing before school, as well as after school. At the weekends, they played all day long. When they got bored of shooting, Romelu found a third player to join them.

'Dad, can Jordan come and play with us too?' he asked. 'I'll look after him, I promise!'

'Please, Dad! Please, please, please!' Jordan begged. He was desperate to join his big brother on the football pitch.

Roger nodded slowly. 'Okay, but if anything happens, there will be BIG trouble.'

'Thanks, Dad!' they shouted behind them as they ran off.

Romelu and Vinnie put Jordan in goal. 'You're the youngest,' they argued. 'We'll let you play out pitch after this game!'

But Romelu and Vinnie's games of one-on-one went on for ages. Whenever one of them was winning, the other changed the rules. 'Okay, next goal wins!'

Eventually, Jordan stopped trying to save their shots.

'Hey, why didn't you stop that?' Romelu shouted.

'I don't want to play in goal anymore!'

'Fine. This time, it really is next goal wins!'

Romelu scored first to set up a match against his brother. He couldn't wait to beat him. 'I hope you're ready to lose!' he teased confidently.

Jordan wasn't scared, though. He was only one year younger than Romelu, even if he was quite a bit smaller. When the game kicked off, he flew straight into the tackle.

'This is going to end in a fight!' Vinnie shouted gleefully.

After a long and tough battle, Romelu was 4-3 up. All he needed was one more goal. Vinnie threw the ball out and he outjumped his brother. He dribbled towards the goal but...

'Romelu! Jordan!'

It was their dad, calling for them to come home. The game stopped.

Romelu pleaded for extra time. 'Dad, we'll just play next goal wins!'

Roger laughed. 'Dinner's on the table and I'm not stupid. I was young once too, you know. If I let you play next goal wins, you'll be here all night! No, you'll just have to wait for a re-match tomorrow.'

CHAPTER 4

LIKE FATHER, LIKE SON

'Wow, what a goal!' Vinnie cheered.

This time, he wasn't talking about one of Romelu's thunder strikes. No, he was talking about one of Romelu's dad's headers. It was a cold, wet day and they were sat inside watching videos of Roger Lukaku's best goals on the internet. When they couldn't play football, watching it was the next best option.

'How does he get so much power on it?' Vinnie asked. 'Whenever I try, it really hurts!'

Romelu didn't know the answer but he knew someone who did. 'Dad!' he called into the kitchen.

When Roger saw what they were watching, he

laughed. 'I'm famous!' he joked. 'That goal was the matchwinner – 2–1 with five minutes to go. That was one of my proudest moments. I was very excited to score but that celebration is unforgivable!'

'Dad, can you please teach us how to head the ball like that?' Romelu asked.

'Yes, Mr Lukaku, how do you do it?' Vinnie added.

'Please, call me Roger... I can certainly give you a few tips. Would you like that?'

'Yes!' Romelu and Vinnie cheered together.

As he looked out of the window, however, Roger changed his mind. It looked really miserable outside. Big puddles were forming in the street, which meant that the grass would be boggy and squelchy. It was nice and warm inside. 'Shall we wait for a day when the weather is a little better?' he suggested hopefully.

The boys shook their heads. 'No, let's go now!' they shouted. For them, the rain suddenly didn't matter anymore.

Roger couldn't disappoint his young fans. Out on their favourite football pitch, he held the ball in his hand. 'Right, the first important thing to learn is what part of the head to use. Do we want to use the top of our head?'

Romelu and Vinnie shook their heads.

'No, we don't! It hurts when the ball hits the top of your head, doesn't it, Vinnie? Also, the ball just goes straight up in the air. What we want to use is our forehead. This part right here! Try it.'

Roger threw the ball up gently and the boys took it in turn to practise. After a few tries, they were both heading it confidently.

'It doesn't hurt at all,' Vinnie said with a smile. 'Thanks, Mr Lukaku!'

'Please, call me Roger! Good, that was step one. Now on to step two – the jump. If you want to score goals, you need to be able to head the ball down. It's much harder for goalkeepers to make saves when you aim low. So, get yourself into a good position and jump high as the ball comes towards you. Try it.'

Romelu leapt up into the air but he was back down on the ground by the time the ball sailed over his head.

'Timing is very important!' Roger laughed. 'When the ball arrives, your head needs to be above it.'

It was Vinnie's turn. He jumped at the right moment, but the ball only brushed his forehead.

'Not bad!' Roger clapped. 'But try to keep your eyes open next time.'

Romelu and Vinnie were having so much fun. They were being coached by a real footballer and it was just the two of them. It became a competition to see who could learn the steps quickest.

'It's easier for you, Rom, because you're so much taller than me!'

'No way, that doesn't make any difference! It's all about technique, isn't it, Dad?'

'You're both doing really well, boys!' Roger called out as he chased after Romelu's header. 'I think you're ready for step three – the direction. For this, you'll need to use your neck muscles but please be very careful. We don't want any injuries!'

An hour later, they were all exhausted and soaked but Romelu and Vinnie were now heading experts. They knew how to use lots of power to score, and they also knew how to delicately flick the ball into the far corner. They couldn't wait to show off their new skills against the other local kids. Vinnie, Romelu and Jordan often took them all on and won, but now they'd be better than ever.

'That was the best training session ever,' Vinnie said, resting on the grass. 'Thanks, Mr Lukaku!'

Romelu's dad rolled his eyes and smiled. 'How many times do I have to tell you? Call me Roger!'

'Ok Mr Luk–, sorry Roger!'

Back at the house, the boys watched the videos of Roger's best goals again.

'Boy, your dad was a really good player!' Vinnie said, his eyes glued to the computer screen. He had a new football hero.

It was the same football hero that Romelu had admired all his young life. 'When I'm older, I want to score lots of goals just like my dad,' he replied proudly.

But heading wasn't the only way to score. Romelu also practised his shooting, with his left foot and with his right foot. He even found time to practise his sprinting with Vinnie too. As he got older, he knew that he would get stronger, but he refused to let that extra muscle slow him down. He wanted to have pace *and* power. If he was good at everything, how could defenders stop him? He never stopped dreaming and working.

Roger was very impressed by his son's attitude. 'If you keep going like this, you're going to be a much better striker than me!' he told him.

That seemed impossible but Romelu would definitely try his best.

CHAPTER 5

RUPEL BOOM

'Wow, that's definitely Roger Lukaku's son,' Erwin
Wosky muttered to himself, trying to hide his
amazement. Romelu had just arrived for his very first
training session with the Rupel Boom Under-7s. 'He's
the tallest six-year-old I've ever seen!'

Thanks to a big diet of food and football, Romelu
stood out head and shoulders above his new
teammates. He was as skinny as a lamppost, shooting
straight up into the late summer sky. There was
nowhere for him to hide on the biggest day of his
life so far. After years of asking his dad about joining
Boom, his wish had come true. He could see the

coaches whispering about 'Roger's son', but the boy was there to make a name for *himself.*

He was glad to have Vinnie there by his side. It was hard to feel too nervous when he was playing football with his best friend. As the session started, they shared a look that said, 'Let's show them what we can do!'

In no time at all, it became The Romelu and Vinnie Show. Vinnie won the ball and played the pass through to Romelu, who sprinted past the defenders and scored. It was a simple game-plan, but it worked every time. On the touchline, the smile kept growing on Erwin's face. He was very impressed, and not just by Romelu's size.

'He's got a bit of work to do on his touch and technique,' the Rupel Boom youth coach noted, 'but that kid could be unstoppable!'

Romelu had so much raw pace and power. Even when he scuffed or sliced his shot, the keeper still couldn't stop it. The other Boom youngsters looked at each other with shock and fear on their faces. What could they do against him?

Romelu was having the time of his life out there. Erwin could see how much he loved scoring and winning. There was hunger in the boy's eyes and he was always calling for the ball. That attitude was very important.

As Romelu and Vinnie left the training pitch together, they laughed and chatted loudly. They were delighted with their victory.

'What a double act!' Erwin said, patting each of them on the back. 'I have a very good feeling about this season.'

Once off the pitch, though, Romelu's confidence suddenly disappeared. 'T-thanks, Coach,' he replied shyly, looking down at the ground and his big feet.

It was the perfect reminder that Romelu was still only a kid. Over the next four years, as the boy developed as a player and a person, Erwin would have to look after his young star carefully. It didn't take long for word to spread about Romelu's incredible goalscoring. Not everyone appreciated his gifts as much as his coach, though, and the parents of his opponents often grew jealous and cruel.

'Referee, that kid's closer to twenty-six than six –
are you blind?'

'This is a joke – they're cheating!'

Thankfully, Erwin was there to defend his star
striker, and so was Adolphine. Roger was often away
playing his own football matches at the weekend,
but Romelu's mum was always there on the
sidelines. She hated to see her son being treated so
badly, just because he was very tall for his age and
scored lots of goals. It was clear discrimination but
every week she carried her son's passport in her bag,
ready for any comments.

'Romelu was born in Belgium and he's six years
old. Here's the proof – now leave him alone!' she
shouted angrily. She was so proud of her children
and protected them fiercely.

Out on the pitch, the horrible comments only
spurred Romelu on to score even more goals.
Nothing could stop him, not even the dirty tackles.
If a player tried to kick him, he just carried on
running. If a player tried to pull his shirt, he just
dragged him along!

There was only one time when Romelu let the nasty talk get to him. Against their biggest rivals, he missed a late chance to win the match.

On the sidelines, the Wilrijk coach laughed. 'Wow, what a clumsy finish. Maybe he is as young as he says he is, after all!'

Romelu was devastated as he trudged off the pitch. He felt like he had let his team down at the crucial moment. But Erwin put an arm around his shoulder. 'Don't worry about that but don't forget either. There will be a next time!'

Those words stayed in Romelu's head for months until the rematch with Wilrijk. He couldn't wait to get his revenge and show the opposition's coach how wrong he was.

'We're going to win this!' Romelu told his teammates in the dressing room before kick-off. His fists were clenched, and he spoke loudly like a leader. His shyness had disappeared.

Erwin had never seen his striker look quite so determined before. 'Those Wilrijk players have no chance today,' he thought to himself happily.

Romelu scored an early goal and the thrashing carried on from there. Even when he got his hat-trick, he didn't slow down. At the final whistle, he had five goals and Rupel Boom celebrated a huge victory.

This time, Romelu left the pitch with his head held high. He looked over at the embarrassed Wilrijk coach and smiled. He was the first of many managers to learn an important lesson – it was a very bad idea to question Romelu's talent.

CHAPTER 6

WINTAM

'Can't I just get a bike?' Romelu pleaded, with tears in his eyes. 'I don't want to move to a different club!'

Roger shook his head sadly. He hated to upset his son, but the family car had broken down and they didn't have enough money to fix it, or to buy a new one. The Rupel Boom training ground was too far away for the boys to walk or cycle there. So Romelu and Jordan would have to play for their local team KFC Wintam instead.

'It's only for now,' his dad promised him. 'At the end of the season, we'll think again, okay?'

Romelu nodded slowly – there was no point

arguing with his dad. He would just have to shine for his new team and then see what happened next.

'Welcome!' Wintam's coach Steve De Buyser said, flashing him a friendly smile. 'It's great to have you here.'

It really was. Steve knew all about Romelu's talent. Everyone in the village did. Rupel Boom's bad luck was Wintam's good luck. Their coach was really looking forward to working with Romelu, for however long he stayed.

'Here you go,' Steve said, throwing him a shirt. 'You're going to look good in green!'

Romelu was like a man amongst boys. Not only was he much taller and faster than his new teammates but he was also better at dribbling and, of course, shooting.

'He's even better than I thought!' Steve thought to himself excitedly.

At the age of ten, Romelu was soon playing for the Wintam Under-13s. His opponents were older and stronger, but he wasn't scared of anything. He raised his game to the next level. If the ball didn't come to him, he would run back to get it. He was scoring more goals than ever in his very own one-boy team.

Steve had never coached a youngster with so much potential. That's why he pushed Romelu to improve his game.

'You've got one of the best left foots I've ever seen, but what about that right foot of yours?'

Romelu shrugged. 'It's pretty good.'

'Well, let's see it then. The defenders in this league know all about your left foot now and they'll try to push you onto your right. If that's good too, then they've got no chance!'

Thanks to his extra work with Vinnie and Jordan, Romelu could kick the ball really powerfully with his right foot. His accuracy, however, needed improvement. With Steve watching, he smashed his shots wide of the posts and over the bar.

'What are you aiming at when you strike the ball?' the Wintam coach asked Romelu.

His student didn't answer.

'You can't just hit it and hope for the best!'

With the target now in his mind, Romelu's right

foot shooting improved. But Steve had an idea to make it even better.

'Give me your boot,' the coach said, pointing and holding out his hand.

'What?' Romelu asked, looking very confused. The team training session was about to begin.

'With lots of hard work and dedication, I believe that you could be a professional footballer one day,' his coach told him. 'Is that what you want?'

Romelu nodded eagerly – he would do whatever it took to achieve that dream.

'Right, so give me your left boot. That way, you'll have no choice but to use your right foot!'

Luckily, the ground was dry, but it still felt weird to play with one boot and one sock. At first, Romelu forgot and controlled the ball with his left foot as usual. He went to shoot, but it trickled towards the goal and hurt his foot.

'Use your right!' Steve reminded him.

Slowly, Romelu got used to shooting with his weaker foot.

'Nice finish!' Steve cheered and threw his left boot

back to him. 'Now, try to keep switching feet. Keep the defender guessing!'

The coaching worked a treat and added yet another strength to Romelu's game. The ten-year-old was a tall, powerful striker who could head the ball and shoot accurately with either foot. Was there anything that could stop him?

'How long have you had those boots?' Steve asked him one day. He could see strips of tape covering up holes. His big left toe was starting to poke through. 'They're falling apart!'

Romelu frowned. 'I haven't had them that long, Coach. Besides, they're my lucky boots. I've scored fifty goals with these this season!'

The Wintam coach knew the truth. Romelu's boots were very old but his family couldn't afford to buy him a new pair.

'Maybe I could do something about that...,' Steve thought to himself.

During a bus journey to France, he sat down next to Romelu. After chatting about football for a while, the Wintam coach took a cardboard box out of his bag. He handed it to Romelu and put his finger to his lips.

As he opened the box, Romelu tried to hide his excitement. Inside was a brand-new pair of football boots! He took them out, studied them carefully and sniffed the fresh shoe smell. He couldn't wait to wear them.

'Thanks,' he whispered to Steve. 'I'm going to be amazing in this tournament now, I promise!'

Romelu kept his word. Wearing his new boots, he scored goal after goal and was named the best player of the tournament.

As they travelled home to Belgium, Romelu thanked his coach again. Steve smiled. 'It's my pleasure – you earned them. Just remember me when you're a world-famous striker!'

CHAPTER 7

SCOUTED

Dirk Gyselinckx was relaxing at home when his phone rang. He groaned – not another call! Why couldn't people leave him in peace for a few minutes? Slowly, the Lierse S.K. youth coach lifted himself out of his chair and picked up.

'Hello, Dirk speaking?'

'Hi there, I hope I haven't caught you at a bad moment. My name is Marck Van Hooymissen and I'm–'

Dirk recognised the name – Marck was one of his sister's friends. 'Yes, I remember. How are you?'

'I'm well, thanks. How are you?'

'Yes, not too bad, thanks,' Dirk replied. That was enough small talk. 'So, how can I help you?'

'Sorry, I'll get to the point. I saw an amazing striker in an Under-12s match in Wintam yesterday. He was so good that I *had* to let you know!'

Dirk had this kind of conversation almost every day. He was always grateful for people's help but 90 per cent of the time, the tips ended in disappointment. When he went to watch an 'incredible young talent', the discovery often either turned out to be a one-trick pony, or the coach's son.

Despite this, Dirk always went along to check. Discovering the next big thing was a long and winding journey. It was exhausting but that amazing moment when you found a unique talent made it all worthwhile.

'What's his name?' the Lierse youth coach asked.

'Romelu Lukaku.'

Dirk knew the surname. He remembered watching the kid's dad, Roger, playing for Rupel Boom. He was a good striker too. 'Thanks, I'll check him out.'

'Great, you won't be disappointed!' Marck told him confidently.

Dirk spotted the 'amazing striker' as soon as he arrived at Wintam's next home game. It wasn't difficult; Romelu towered over everyone else. 'Wow, he's a big kid!' he said to himself.

Still, Dirk was ready to be disappointed. Lots of big kids did well in the younger age groups but then faded away when everyone else grew up. Did Romelu have the talent to match his size? The youth coach couldn't wait to find out.

Wintam's game-plan was clear right from the start – hoof the ball up the pitch for Romelu to chase and score. It was very simple, but the opposition defenders weren't quick or strong enough to stop him. Every time they tried to tackle him, he dribbled straight through them.

'That kid is far too good for this league,' Dirk thought to himself. 'He needs a proper challenge.'

By the end of the match, Romelu had another five goals and another interested scout. After speaking to Steve, the Wintam coach, Dirk went over to introduce himself to the star striker and his parents.

'What a performance, Romelu! My name is Dirk and I work at the Lierse S.K. youth academy,' he began. 'We're always looking for great young players and your son really fits the bill. We'd love for him to come down and train with us. What do you think?'

A few minutes later, the deal was done. But Dirk didn't leave with one new player; he left with three! Vinnie and Jordan would also be joining Romelu at Lierse.

'We're on our way to the big time!' Romelu told his best friends happily.

Romelu couldn't wait to step up to the next level. From the very first minute of the very first training session, he worked hard to impress his new coaches. He had to prove himself all over again.

Romelu went straight into the Lierse starting line-up and he never lost his place. In the end, the simple Wintam game-plan didn't change. It didn't need to. The opponents were better but as soon as Romelu sprinted forward, they got scared. At full speed, no-one could catch him.

Despite all of his amazing performances, there were still people who doubted Romelu's ability:

'He's only good because he's bigger than everyone else!'

'Just wait until everyone else is his size – he'll be rubbish!'

It was a good thing that Romelu was used to the cruel comments. They only made him more determined to keep improving and become a top professional footballer. That would definitely shut them up!

Thanks to lots of extra practice, his ball control and footwork were getting better and better. Even when three or four defenders surrounded him, they still couldn't get the ball off him.

'That's it, great hold-up play, Rom!' Dirk cheered on the touchline. He was very pleased with his signing. Even at such a young age, Romelu was very ambitious. He loved learning new things and developing his game. With an attitude like that, Dirk believed that he could go on to fulfil that incredible potential.

'Mark my words – Romelu is the future of Belgian football!' he told everyone who would listen.

After two great seasons and 121 goals, it was time for Romelu to leave Lierse behind. But where would he go next?

'I've been offered a job at Anderlecht,' Dirk told him. Anderlecht were Belgium's biggest and best football team. They won the league almost every season. 'And I want you and Jordan to come with me.'

It was an incredible opportunity for the Lukaku brothers, but what about Vinnie? Could they really leave their best friend behind?

Luckily, Vinnie wasn't surprised by the news. 'Congratulations!' he told them. 'I always knew that you guys would go all the way to the top. Just promise me one thing: when you become international superstars, you'll still hang out with your oldest friend. Promise?'

'Promise!'

CHAPTER 8

HARD WORK AT ANDERLECHT

'This is so cool!' Jordan said excitedly as a big, shiny people-carrier pulled up outside their house in Wintam. Lots of their neighbours were at their windows, watching the scene. 'It's like we're famous already!'

Anderlecht had sent the car to pick them up and take them to training. It was a pretty nice way to travel. The car had comfortable leather seats with lots of legroom. Compared to the old family car that had broken down, it was total luxury. Romelu spent the forty-minute journey trying to control his brother's excitement.

'Put your feet down! Your trainers are dirty.'

'Can you please just sit still? What's wrong with you? You're not five years old anymore!'

Jordan did as he was told but then moved straight on to a new idea. 'Can we change the radio station please?' he asked the driver. 'This music is rubbish!'

Romelu was very glad when the car finally pulled up at the Anderlecht academy centre. At least his brother had helped to take his mind off the big night ahead. Now, as he looked up at the huge 'RSCA' sign, Romelu's heart began to beat a lot faster. It was time for him to take on his biggest challenge yet.

'How are you feeling?' Jordan asked him.

Romelu had his game face on. 'Ready,' he replied quietly but confidently.

They got out and walked over to the entrance, where Dirk was waiting to welcome them to Anderlecht. 'Great, you made it! This is our youth technical director, Jean Kindermans.'

Jean gave them each a firm handshake. 'Nice to meet you – I've heard great things about you boys!'

After a quick tour of the facilities, it was time for the main event – training. Jordan could be very annoying at times but Romelu was still glad to have his brother there with him. The new kids sat next to each other in the changing room, as the other players joked around together.

'Don't worry, you're the biggest kid here by a mile!' Jordan whispered.

Romelu nodded but he knew that size alone wouldn't make him a successful footballer at the top level. The other Anderlecht youngsters were smaller, but their technique was brilliant. They could all control the ball perfectly, move the ball quickly and spot clever passes. It was amazing to watch. As they waited for their turns in the first passing drill, Romelu and Jordan shared a look of fear. Were they really good enough to play for the best club in Belgium?

'Try to cushion the ball more with your first touch,' Jean explained patiently. 'Don't give the defender the chance to come in and steal it.'

Romelu knew that he had a lot to learn but he was desperate to become a better player. If that meant adapting his style, he didn't mind at all. Romelu wouldn't be chasing after long balls all game anymore, like he had at Wintam and Lierse. That wasn't the Anderlecht way. Instead, he would need to be able to pass the ball around and join in with the flowing, attacking football.

'It might take me a few sessions to get up to speed, but I'll be banging in the goals in no time!' he promised Dirk at the end of their tough first practice.

'Don't worry, I believe you!' his coach replied. He had learnt never to doubt Romelu.

The Lukaku brothers had a lot to think about on their car journey home. Jordan was so exhausted that he stayed quiet for twenty whole minutes.

'That was hard, bro!' he admitted eventually. 'We've got work to do if we're going to catch up with those other kids. They might look young, but they play like they've been doing this forever.'

Romelu nodded. It wasn't going to be easy, but he wouldn't let anything get in the way of his dream. He just needed to make a plan...

That plan would have to wait, though, because Jordan had found some extra energy. 'Could you turn the music up please? I love this song!'

Romelu kept his promise to Dirk. Thanks to lots of hard work on the training pitch, he was soon banging in nearly as many goals for the Anderlecht youth team as he had for his other clubs. He proved that no challenge was too big for him.

Jean was delighted with the progress. 'I'm not sure which of you was the better signing – you or Rom!' he told Dirk.

'And don't forget about Jordan,' he reminded. 'The three of us together must count as Anderlecht's best signing ever!'

It was hard to argue with that. Romelu was on track to become one of the club's top young players. Even at the age of fourteen, people were talking about the bright future ahead of him. But Romelu didn't get carried away. Instead of relaxing, he became even more serious about football. If he wanted to become a top professional, he needed to act like one.

'Look at this muscleman!' Dirk joked when he saw him on the training ground. 'Is that a six-pack? You used to be all skin and bones. What happened?'

The answer was that Romelu was eating well and exercising well. His days started with sit-ups, press-ups and ab work in his bedroom. After a shower and a healthy breakfast, he ran the three miles to school with Jordan. In the evenings, he trained at Anderlecht, then went home, ate dinner, did his stretches, and went to bed. It was a tiring routine, but Romelu was adding power without losing pace.

'Just don't wear yourself out, okay?' Adolphine warned him. 'If I hear that you're falling asleep in class, there will be BIG trouble.'

CHAPTER 9

PURPLE TALENTS

'Education is the most important thing,' Roger told his sons again and again as they were growing up. 'If you study hard you could go to university and get really good jobs. That would make me so proud!'

Romelu liked school but he liked football even more. 'My grades are good, Papa. Can't I study hard *and* play hard?'

Roger just wanted the best for his children. Playing football was a lot of fun, but it wasn't necessarily a good career choice. Roger knew that from his own experience at Rupel Boom. Lots of very good players didn't make it to the top level. Even if Romelu did, one bad injury could ruin everything. His son was balancing his education and football well so far, but Anderlecht was a long way from his school and home in Wintam.

'At Lille, the kids move into the academy facilities,' Roger told Jean and Dirk at a meeting about Romelu's future. 'That way, they can live, study and train in the same place. That makes a lot of sense to me. Look at Eden Hazard – it's working for him, isn't it?'

Dirk nodded. It was sad to see Belgium's top young talents moving away to France and England because of better opportunities. The only way for Anderlecht to stop that happening was to improve their academy system. It was too basic and old-fashioned. Keeping hold of Romelu was a very good reason for change.

'Roger, I agree, and we want your sons to be happy here,' Dirk replied. 'That's our number one aim, I promise. Just give us a bit of time, and we'll find an answer.'

The answer was a brand-new youth programme called 'Purple Talents'. Romelu and Jordan were the first members. They moved schools to the Saint-Guidon Institute in Brussels, which was much closer to the club's training centre.

'Everything is so much easier now,' Romelu told his dad happily. 'There's much less boring travel time.'

'I'm glad to hear that,' Roger replied. 'But don't forget about your studies!'

He was right to worry because Romelu was playing more football than ever. Under the new system, Anderlecht's academy players now trained seven times a week. There were even one-on-one coaching sessions, which Romelu loved. With the extra attention, he could really focus on improving his technique. In a crowded penalty area, he needed to react more quickly, control the ball better, and shoot more accurately. He was determined to get it right, no matter how long it took.

'Come on, that's enough for today,' the coach said, looking at his watch. They had already done an extra hour and it was getting dark. 'Go home, get some dinner and get some rest!'

Despite all the goals that he scored, Romelu still worried about every miss. He aimed for perfection in every performance, even when that wasn't possible.

'No way, you can't call that a miss,' Dirk tried to tell him. 'The keeper made a great save, and we still won 5 1!'

Romelu would stay in a bad mood for a few hours but eventually he always moved on to thinking about the next match, and the next chance to score.

'Rom is turning sixteen soon,' Jean reminded Dirk for the hundredth time. The date was there in big letters on his wall calendar: 13 May 2009. 'Could you ask Roger to come in for another meeting please?'

Anderlecht weren't the only club who wanted to offer Romelu his first professional contract. Thanks to his incredible goalscoring record, he was a target for all of the top teams in Europe. There were crowds of scouts watching every game he played.

Luckily for Anderlecht, Romelu's dad wasn't interested in the big money offers, however. He just wanted his son to enjoy his football. He knew that Romelu loved playing for Anderlecht. The club looked after him well and really cared about his development as a player.

'As you know, everyone here thinks the world of Romelu,' Jean explained at the big meeting. 'He's going to be a star – there's no question about that! He's already training with the first team, which is great experience for him, but we're not going to rush things. He needs time and he needs support. That's why Anderlecht is the best place for Romelu at this stage of his career.'

Roger didn't need much persuading. 'Thank you, let's hope that Rom can repay you with some goals in the first team!' he laughed as they agreed a deal until 2012. All that was missing now was the sixteen-year-old's signature.

'Good to see you!' Jean said, shaking Romelu's hand and welcoming him into his office. 'Here's the contract. Take your time, and when you're happy, sign at the bottom of each page.'

In a flash, Romelu scribbled his name at the bottom of each page. 'Thanks!' he said as he rushed out of the door.

He trusted his dad's judgement and, more importantly, he had a training session to go to. Romelu was getting closer and closer to making his Anderlecht debut. When it came to playing football, he didn't want to miss a single minute.

CHAPTER 10

DREAM DEBUT?

On a Sunday morning two weeks later, Vinnie walked over to the Lukaku house in Wintam and knocked on the front door. He was looking forward to a fun day with Romelu – watching football on TV, playing FIFA on the PlayStation, and playing football on their favourite pitch.

But it was his mum who answered. 'Hi Vinnie, how are you?'

'I'm good thanks, Mrs Lukaku. Is Rom awake yet?'

Adolphine looked confused. 'Didn't he tell you? He's gone to Liège!'

Of course, how had Vinnie forgotten? Anderlecht were playing away at Standard Liège for the chance to win the Belgian league title. The score in the home leg was 1-1, so the Purple and Whites needed a victory. Romelu must have been given a ticket for the game.

'Cool! Does he get to sit down near the dugout?' Vinnie asked.

Adolphine still looked confused. 'Really, he didn't tell you? He's one of the substitutes!'

Vinnie couldn't believe it. Romelu was about to play the biggest match of his life and he hadn't said a word to his best friend! But it wasn't the right time to get angry or hurt. Instead, Vinnie got excited.

'Wow, how's he feeling?' he asked.

Adolphine laughed. 'You know what Rom's like – he doesn't know what nerves are. He can't wait!'

Even in his dreams, Romelu hadn't expected to make his Anderlecht debut at the age of sixteen. He wasn't old enough to drive a car; he hadn't even finished school yet. But there he was, entering the dressing room with all of the senior players to get ready for their biggest match of the season. It felt too good to be true.

Romelu had been training with the senior squad

for months but he still didn't feel totally relaxed around them. As an Anderlecht fan, these men were his heroes, the players that he looked up to. Alongside experienced international footballers from Belgium, the Czech Republic, Poland, Morocco and Argentina, Romelu was learning all the time.

'No, this *is* true!' he told himself. There was a purple shirt laid out for him – '36 LUKAKU'. He couldn't wait to wear it with pride.

If Standard Liège scored first, Anderlecht would need goals quickly. That was the team's biggest problem. Only midfielder Mbark Boussoufa had scored more than ten goals during the season. Meanwhile in the youth team, Romelu had scored 131 in 93 games. Playing in the Belgian Pro League would be a completely different challenge, but he had proved that he was a natural finisher.

'Are you ready for this?' the manager, Ariel Jacobs, asked, putting an arm around his shoulder.

Romelu nodded confidently. 'Of course, Coach – just bring me on and I'll score!'

Near the end of the first half, Standard Liège

took the lead with a penalty. On the bench, Romelu looked glum but it wasn't all bad news. In order to win, Anderlecht would now need to bring on a goalscorer like him. The change didn't happen at half-time but a few minutes into the second half, Jacobs told him to warm up.

Romelu jumped out of his seat and started doing his stretches. The Anderlecht fans cheered loudly as he jogged past. They were already excited about the club's 'next big thing'.

With thirty minutes to go, Romelu stood on the touchline, ready to become an Anderlecht hero.

'If you get a chance, don't rush it,' his manager told him. 'Go out there and cause them some problems!'

With his dreadlocks flapping, Romelu raced on to the field. This was his moment! The adrenaline rushed through his body as he chased after the ball. When he got it on the right, Romelu only had one thought on his mind – attack. He ran at the left-back and with a lovely stepover, he dribbled straight past him. All that extra work on his technique had really paid off.

The Anderlecht supporters were up on their feet, waiting. What would their young superstar do next? Sadly, his cross flew just over Tom De Sutter's head.

'Come on!' the fans shouted, urging their team on. Romelu's energy and skill had given them a new hope of victory.

Romelu kept going but the Standard Liège defence stood strong. At the final whistle, Romelu left the field feeling very disappointed. Yes, he had made his Anderlecht debut, but it hadn't been the incredible debut that he had hoped for. It hadn't been the match-winning debut that he had dreamt about so many times as a young child. He hadn't scored, and Anderlecht hadn't won the league. He hated losing more than anything in the world.

'Well done, son,' Roger said, giving him a comforting hug. 'You did your best. Next year, you'll be Anderlecht's number-one striker and you'll lead them to the title.'

Yet again, Romelu was very grateful for his dad's support. He never stopped believing in his son's talent. When the Belgium Under-16s coach said that

Romelu would only get into his team as a left-winger, Roger shook his head.

'No, my son is a goalscorer!' he explained firmly. 'He's a central striker. If you think you have a better striker in your team, then don't pick him. But don't play him out of position on the wing.'

It didn't take Romelu long to prove his Under-16s coach wrong.

Belgium's best young goalscorer couldn't wait for the 2009–10 season to begin. Romelu's debut against Standard Liège had been a first taste of action. He was now hungry for more.

He pushed himself harder than ever in preseason training to make sure that he was 100 per cent ready to shine. As soon as his free Anderlecht season tickets arrived, they were gone. He gave three to his family, one to Vinnie, and one to Steve, his old Wintam coach.

'Thanks for everything. I'll never forget you, or those boots!' Romelu wrote in the card. Soon, he would be a world-famous striker, just as Steve had predicted.

CHAPTER 11

RISING STAR

As Mbark dribbled in from the left wing, Romelu ran towards the front post. 'Yes!' he shouted, calling for the cross.

The Zulte Waregem centre-back was marking him closely but Romelu stretched out his long leg first and flicked the ball straight through the goalkeeper's legs.

Goooooooooooooooooooooaaaaaaaaaaaaaaaaaaaaaallll lllllllllllllllllllllllllllllll!!!!!!!!!!!

Romelu was off the mark! He sprinted towards the corner and jumped the advertising boards to celebrate with the Anderlecht fans behind the fence. He had scored his first senior goal for the club and it felt absolutely amazing. There was no feeling like it.

'I could take on the world right now!' Romelu screamed to Mbark with a look of pure joy on his face.

It was Anderlecht's fourth league match of the season, and Romelu had only been on the field for twenty minutes.

'Hopefully, I won't be a super sub for much longer,' he told his family.

A few weeks later, Romelu got his wish. He was named in the starting line-up for their home match against Gent. All of his favourite people were there in the Constant Vanden Stock Stadium to watch him – his parents, Jordan, Vinnie, Steve, and, of course, the other 20,000 Anderlecht fans.

Romelu had several good chances but for once, he failed to score. Every time he took a shot, a defender blocked it. Every time a cross came into the box, it went just past his foot or head. He was substituted with five minutes to go.

'Don't worry,' Jacobs told him as he trudged off the pitch. 'It just wasn't your day today. You'll bounce back in the next game.'

Romelu had a big point to prove when he came on

in the second half against Excelsior Mouscron. Just because he was still only seventeen, it didn't mean that he couldn't be Anderlecht's top goalscorer in the Belgian Pro League. He just needed a little more experience and a bit of luck.

With fifteen minutes to go, an Anderlecht defender booted it downfield from inside his own penalty area. Romelu was on to it in a flash. It was like he was back at Lierse, chasing after long balls again. There were two defenders around him, but he was far too quick and strong for them. As he dribbled into the penalty area, he slowed down. He didn't want to rush his shot and waste another glorious chance to score. As the goalkeeper went right, Romelu went left.

Goooooooooooooaaaaaaaaaaaaaaaaaaaaalllllllllllllll llllllllllllll!!!!!!!!!!!!!!!!!!!!

2-1 to Anderlecht! Romelu was in a good mood now. He ran towards the halfway line with his tongue hanging out, and pulled funny faces in front of the TV camera.

'That's our boy!' Roger and Adolphine cheered in

the stands. Soon, all of the grateful fans around them were asking to shake their hands.

What Anderlecht needed was a consistent, goalscoring striker. Romelu was determined to be that striker. Against Charleroi, he scored another beauty. This time, as the keeper went low, Romelu went high. His shot rocketed into the top corner.

Goooooooooooaaaaaaaaaaaaaaaaaaaaalllllllllllllllllllllll llllllllll!!!!!!!!!!!!!!!!!!!!!!!

It was time for Romelu to show off his cool new celebration. As the crowd went wild, he did a cartwheel and then a backflip. When he landed, he beat his heart with his fist and roared. Scoring for Anderlecht meant so much to him. It was very entertaining but on the touchline, Jacobs could hardly watch. The last thing the manager needed was an injury to his Golden Boy.

'Please don't do that again!' he begged.

Romelu was on a roll and he reached double figures in January 2010 as Anderlecht thrashed their rivals, Standard Liège, 4–0. His goal was a powerful header that even his dad would have been proud of.

'Revenge is sweet!' Romelu laughed with his teammates.

His breakthrough season was going very well indeed. Anderlecht were top of the Belgian Pro League and they were doing well in the Europa League too. They beat Ajax 3–1 and Athletic Bilbao 4–0. Romelu, of course, was on target in both matches. 'Lukaku-mania' was taking over Belgium.

'We need him in the national team now!' the fans urged.

Romelu had only played a few matches for the Under-21s but why wait? He was ready! In February, Dick Advocaat named him in the senior squad for the friendly against Croatia.

'You two are our future,' the Belgium manager told Romelu and Lille attacker Eden Hazard.

For the first time in a long time, Romelu felt a little overwhelmed. He was very proud to wear the red, black and yellow shirt but 'the future of Belgian football'? That was a lot of pressure at such a young age, especially when he hadn't even made his international debut yet. Despite their best efforts,

Romelu and Eden couldn't lead their country to victory against Croatia.

'Never mind, we've got plenty of years ahead of us!' Eden said afterwards.

Romelu turned his focus back to club football. He had a first major trophy to win. This time, Anderlecht won the play-offs and collected their thirtieth league title. It was just as his dad had predicted. In the space of twelve amazing months, Romelu had gone from making his debut to becoming the team's star striker.

'We could be playing in the Champions League next season,' he told Mbark excitedly as they watched the big fireworks display in the Constant Vanden Stock Stadium. 'That would be so cool!'

Once the title celebrations were over, Romelu felt exhausted. What a year it had been. At the age of seventeen, he was already a league title winner, an international footballer *and* the top scorer in Belgium. What he needed now was a long rest.

'I think we should hide you away for the summer,' Jean joked. 'It's great that you're getting goals, but the big clubs are circling like sharks!'

As Europe's hottest young talent, Romelu would soon have big decisions to make about his future. Where would he go next? Real Madrid? Barcelona? Juventus? AC Milan? Or his favourite childhood club, Chelsea?

CHAPTER 12

CHELSEA DREAM PART I

Romelu's love of Chelsea had started when he was only seven years old. It was a weekend family tradition to watch the big Premier League matches on TV at home. That afternoon, it was Manchester United vs Chelsea.

Early on in the game Chelsea's Dutch striker, Jimmy Floyd Hasselbaink, chested the ball down on the edge of the penalty area. As the defenders ran out to close him down, Hasselbaink smashed it into the back of the net. The United goalkeeper didn't even move. 1-0!

'What a goal!' Romelu cheered. The replays made it look even better.

His dad laughed and rolled his eyes. 'Let me guess – you're a Chelsea fan now?'

'That's right!' Romelu replied and he never changed his mind.

His support grew even stronger when The Blues signed Didier Drogba four years later. Drogba quickly became Romelu's idol, his favourite player to watch. The Ivorian was the complete striker. He was strong *and* quick, and he could score every type of goal.

Romelu had a Drogba poster on his bedroom wall and two '11 DROGBA' Chelsea shirts – one to sleep in and one to play football in. He watched videos of the striker's best goals all the time. *'Drogbaaaaaaaaaa aaaaaaaaaaaaaaaaaaaaaaaaaa!!!!!!!'*

Whenever he scored a goal, Romelu copied Drogba's goal celebrations. He even got the same Nike boots that Drogba wore.

'I'm going to be just like Didier when I'm older!' he told Vinnie.

As he grew up, people often said that Romelu had a similar playing style to his hero. They were both big, strong strikers who scored lots of goals. Romelu was very proud of the comparison. It was a massive honour.

'If I could be half as good as him, I'll be happy,' he told his dad.

Roger shook his head. 'Nonsense, you've got to aim higher than that. You'll be better than Drogba. How many World Cups has he won?'

'None.'

'Exactly.'

ʌ

Chelsea first started scouting Romelu when he was only twelve years old. Their Sporting Director, Frank Arnesen, was on a mission to sign the best young players from all over the world. Chelsea wanted the stars of the future, as well as the present. 'Lukaku' was a name that Arnesen kept hearing. In the end, he sent his son Sebastien to Belgium to watch him play.

'So, what did you think?' Arnesen asked him afterwards.

Sebastien was full of praise. 'Dad, that kid is going to be a star! He's huge but he's got real talent too.

The goalkeeper couldn't even get close to his shots!'

'What about his attitude?'

'It seems good to me. He works hard for the team and he's not a hothead. The defenders were kicking him and pulling his shirt, but he just kept going.'

Chelsea took their time. Over the next few years, club scouts watched videos of every single one of Romelu's matches for the Anderlecht youth teams. They studied his performances carefully, and even spoke to his school teachers. They wanted to know everything about their future signing.

'Rom is a good kid,' they said. 'No, he doesn't strut around like he's already a star. When he's here, he's just a normal student!'

That was exactly what Chelsea were looking for – dedicated young players, not arrogant show-offs.

'He's getting better and better,' the scouts reported. 'Shouldn't we act now? Manchester United and Juventus are watching him too!'

But still, Chelsea watched and waited. They wanted to be 100 per cent sure about Romelu's talent. It was only during his amazing 2009–10 season when Arnesen returned to agree a transfer fee with Anderlecht.

When he heard the news, Romelu was delighted. His dream move was almost complete. He couldn't wait to become a Chelsea player, and learn as much as he could from Didier. Not everyone was so pleased, however.

'No, you can't leave!' his brother pleaded. Jordan was so upset that he paused their FIFA game. 'We haven't played together in the Anderlecht first team yet. That's what we agreed on one of those car journeys back to Wintam, remember?'

The Lukaku brothers had just moved into a cool new flat in Brussels. They were enjoying the chance to live away from home together for the first time. There were no parents around to tell them to clear up their mess, or keep the noise down. Jordan wasn't ready for the fun to end so soon.

'Yeah, it'll be rubbish without you,' Vinnie added. He was a regular visitor at the flat. 'Stay a bit longer!'

In the end, that's exactly what happened. Romelu's

transfer broke down when Arnesen went to discuss it with Roman Abramovich.

'You want to sign a seventeen-year-old for £2 million?' the Chelsea chairman asked. The club never paid that kind of money for such a young player.

'Trust me, he's worth it. He's a beast! He scored fifteen goals last season and he's only just getting started. He's going to be the next Drogba. If not even better!'

Arnesen tried and tried but he couldn't persuade Abramovich. Chelsea's Sporting Director was very disappointed, but he didn't give up.

Neither did Romelu. His dream move could wait a year or two. During the summer break, he went to London on a school trip. On the last day, his class did a stadium tour of Stamford Bridge. Wearing his '11 DROGBA' shirt, Romelu walked around like a kid in a sweet shop.

'This place is amazing!' he said, looking around at the shiny trophies and the huge pictures of Chelsea legends.

While his mates went to explore the dressing rooms, Romelu stayed on the pitch. He bent down to touch the perfect grass. It was like a soft carpet. He didn't have a football, but he imagined playing there, partnering Didier up front. He imagined wearing the famous blue Chelsea shirt, and the roar of the crowd as they scored goal after goal together.

'I'm going to play here one day,' Romelu told his teacher. He was deadly serious. He would make sure of it.

CHAPTER 13

CHELSEA DREAM
PART II

When he returned for preseason training at
Anderlecht, Romelu didn't complain or sulk. He was
too professional to behave like that.

'It's fine, my Chelsea dream can wait,' he told
Jordan.

Romelu focused on making the most of another
season in Belgium. It gave him more time to improve
his game and gain experience.

Number one on Romelu's wish-list was playing
in the Champions League. That's where all the top
strikers played, including Didier. After winning
the Belgian title, Anderlecht were through to the

qualifying rounds of the tournament. Romelu and co were too good for Welsh team The New Saints FC, but they lost on penalties to Serbian side Partizan Belgrade. Romelu was devastated.

'Chin up, son,' Roger told him. 'You'll be playing in the Champions League next season.'

Romelu hoped that his dad was right. He had been right many times before.

Until then, Romelu just wanted to score as many goals as possible. Against Sint-Truiden, he got the ball in the penalty area with his back to goal. After a good first touch, he spun quickly and shot into the bottom corner.

Gooooooooooooooooooooooaaaaaaaaaaaaaaaaaalllllll lllllllllllllllllllll!!!!!!!!!!!!!!!

What a classic striker's goal! Romelu was extra pleased because it was a move that he had worked on with coach René Peeters. He did it so many times in training that he started doing it in his sleep.

'Practice makes perfect!' he thought to himself.

Romelu was being marked more carefully now, but with his strength and speed, he could create space out of nothing. His second goal of the game was all about power. After a neat one-two, he pulled back his amazing left foot and smashed the ball into the roof of the net. The goalkeeper just lay down on the grass, looking confused.

'I'm surprised that shot didn't break the goal!' Mbark joked as he hugged his huge teammate.

The Anderlecht players now relied on Romelu to be their main matchwinner. At the age of eighteen, he couldn't be the hero every time, but he was becoming much more consistent. He enjoyed his new responsibility. His goals against KVC Westerlo, Racing Genk, AA Gent and Zulte Waregem turned draws into wins.

'Those are my favourite goals,' Romelu told Jordan. 'The really important ones!'

If Romelu wanted to be a world-class striker, he needed to score in the biggest games, when the pressure was really on. He was constantly setting himself new targets. After scoring fifteen goals in 2009–10, he reached twenty in 2010–11.

'Progress,' Romelu told his dad happily. He could

feel himself getting better and better. Now, he wanted to test himself at a higher level.

Romelu had become the star for his country as well as for his club. In a friendly against Russia in November 2010, he scored both of Belgium's goals. The first was a simple tap-in but the second was a trademark strike. As a long ball bounced down in the penalty area, he muscled his way past the centre-back and then fired past the goalkeeper. He made it look so easy.

Gooooooooooooooooooooooaaaaaaaaaaaaaaaallllll //////////////////////!!!!!!!!!!!!

Now that he had scored his first international goals, Romelu was hungry for more. His partnership with Eden was growing into something very special. Before too long, they would be teammates at club level too.

*

Even though Frank Arnesen wasn't at Chelsea anymore, the club's interest in Romelu continued. The scouts kept watching videos of his Anderlecht performances and the new Sporting Director Michael

Emenalo was equally impressed by the young striker.

'We should have signed him last summer,' he moaned to the Chelsea scouts. '£2 million was a total bargain – he'll cost a lot more now!'

After two excellent seasons, Romelu had proved that he wasn't a risky signing at all. He wasn't a typical eighteen-year-old; he was guaranteed goals. This time, Abramovich agreed to the transfer, even when Anderlecht asked for a deal worth up to £17 million.

'You're good but you're not *that* good!' Jordan teased. Despite his rude comments, though, he was going to miss his big brother a lot.

Romelu was full of excitement as he travelled to London again. This time, he wasn't visiting as a student; he was arriving as a professional footballer.

'Let's get this started!' he cheered in the taxi from the airport. He was buzzing.

After a long medical at the training ground in Cobham, Romelu was officially announced as a Chelsea player in the summer of 2011. It was a very proud moment as he stood with his new manager

André Villas-Boas and fellow new signing Oriol
Romeu. Wearing a bright blue Adidas tracksuit,
Romelu held up his '18 LUKAKU' shirt for the
cameras.

'It's a dream come true,' he told the English media
with a smile on his face. 'I've wanted to play for
Chelsea since I was a little kid. It's a football club
that's big with lots of ambition – just like me!'

The next question was about Drogba. He answered:
'I'm here to play with him, not replace him! I can't
wait to learn from him. He has so much experience
and he has won everything. He's my idol.'

It had been difficult to leave Anderlecht and his
family behind, but Romelu was ready for a fresh new
start. He was looking forward to his next massive
challenge – competing with Drogba, Nicolas Anelka
and Fernando Torres for a place in the Chelsea
starting line-up.

'I know I'm young but I'm not here to sit on the
bench,' he told Villas-Boas. 'I'm here to score goals!'

CHAPTER 14

SLOW START

'When you shoot, keep your eyes on the ball for as long as possible,' Didier explained to Romelu. Chelsea's two big strikers had stayed behind after the main training session to do some extra finishing exercises. 'That way, you keep your head nice and steady.'

Every day was a school day for Romelu at Chelsea. He was learning so much from Didier and other senior players like Nicolas Anelka, Frank Lampard and captain John Terry.

'If you ever need me, just give me a call,' John said when Romelu arrived at the club. He was too shocked to even say thanks. He now had John Terry's phone number!

At first, Romelu felt very nervous in the Chelsea dressing room. He was new, and he was still only eighteen years old. He decided that it was best to stay quiet, at least for the first few days. But Romelu soon got his confidence back, thanks to his friendly teammates.

'You're doing well!' Didier kept telling him.

Romelu was picked as a substitute for Chelsea's second home match of the 2011–12 season. Sitting on the bench, he was impatient to get out there and play. When Didier went up for a header, Romelu moved his head too. When Fernando took a shot, Romelu moved his leg too. He was desperate to make his debut at Stamford Bridge.

With thirty minutes to go, Villas-Boas sent Nicolas on to replace Didier. Romelu's heart sank. Was that his chance gone? But a few minutes later, he got the call to warm up.

Wearing a bright pink bib, Romelu jogged up and down the touchline, doing his final stretches. Some fans clapped him, but it wasn't the loud reaction that he was used to at Anderlecht. It was early days, though. A few good goals and Romelu would become a Chelsea hero.

As he tucked his shirt in, Villas-Boas gave him his final instructions. 'The Norwich defenders are tired. There's lots of space for you to run into. Use your speed and get us a third goal!'

After a high-five with Fernando, Romelu ran on to the field. He was determined to make a good first impression. He controlled the ball, dribbled forward and then played a simple pass. So far, so good.

In those final ten minutes, Romelu was everywhere. He called for the ball, flicked it on and then made another run into space. When Nicolas crossed from the right, Romelu flung himself forward for the diving header. It flew just wide of the post.

'Next time,' he thought as he picked himself up and ran back into position.

It was disappointing not to score, but at least Chelsea had won the match. Overall, Romelu was pleased with his debut. He just hoped that he had done enough to get more game-time.

But it didn't turn out that way. As the season went on, Romelu got *less* game-time. In some matches, he didn't even make the bench.

'Villas-Boas thinks I'm a gamble but I'm not!' he complained to Didier. 'I just need a good run of games, that's all. I'm new to English football. They can't just throw me in the team for one game and expect me to score a hat-trick. Form doesn't work like that!'

Romelu played in all three of Chelsea's League Cup fixtures, but he didn't score a single goal. He was desperate to get off the mark. In May 2012, he finally got his first Premier League start on the last day of the season against Blackburn Rovers, but he was replaced by Didier after fifty-four minutes.

'What did I do wrong?' Romelu asked his hero after the game. He had set up John's opening goal with a brilliant cross. He had missed one chance, but it was a difficult angle...

'Nothing, you did well,' Didier reassured him. 'Just be patient!'

That really wasn't Romelu's style. As an ambitious

young striker, this slow start was killing him. He was closer to the Chelsea Reserves than their Champions League team. He felt like he was moving backwards.

'Have I made a mistake, Papa?' he asked on the phone. 'I know I'm still young, but I played nearly a hundred first-team matches at Anderlecht! Why don't they trust me? Why did they sign me?'

Roger's response was the same as Didier's. 'Just be patient, son! Drogba, Torres and Anelka are three of the best strikers in the world. Your time will come.'

Chelsea finished the 2011–12 season with two massive matches – the FA Cup Final against Liverpool, and then the Champions League Final against German giants Bayern Munich. Against the odds, the Blues won both finals, thanks to Didier's goals.

'Well done, bro!' Romelu cheered, hugging his hero. He was really pleased for Didier, who had just scored the winning penalty in the shoot-out in Munich. Chelsea were the Champions of Europe!

Romelu joined in with all the joyful celebrations, but he didn't want to touch the trophies.

'No thanks,' he said as Salomon Kalou tried to pass him the Champions League trophy on the team bus.

Romelu didn't feel like he deserved it. He hadn't played in either final. He hadn't even been selected on the bench for either match.

'I just want to play regular football next season,' he told his brother and Vinnie. Belgium hadn't qualified for Euro 2012, so Romelu was enjoying a relaxing summer break.

'What if the new Chelsea manager doesn't think you're ready yet?' Jordan asked him.

'Then I'll go somewhere else on loan,' he replied firmly. 'I didn't leave Anderlecht for this. I'm better than that!'

Romelu wasn't going to sit on the bench and wait any longer. He wanted to win top trophies properly and lift them high into the sky. The first step was getting back to what he did best – scoring lots of goals. Without goals, he felt sad and lost, especially in London, away from his family and friends.

Luckily, Romelu had made a new best friend in England, who was inspiring him to dream big.

CHAPTER 15

ROMELU & PAUL

Romelu first heard about Paul Pogba when he was
fifteen years old. He would never forget the day that
his brother returned home after a game against the
French club Le Havre.

'How did it go?' Romelu asked Jordan.

He shook his head and slumped down onto the
sofa. 'It was awful, we got hammered!'

Their dad had been there watching the match.
'Le Havre had this amazing central midfielder. He
controlled everything – that kid is going to be a top
player one day!'

Romelu rarely heard his dad talk about a player
like that. He was curious – perhaps he would be able

to find YouTube videos of this amazing midfielder.
'What's his name?' he asked.

'Paul Pogba.'

*

Four years later, both youngsters were in England –
Romelu was at Chelsea, and Paul was at Manchester
United. They weren't getting much game-time,
however. As their teams battled it out at Stamford
Bridge, Romelu and Paul were sat in the freezing
cold stands, watching and wishing that they were
out on the pitch. It was a frustrating time for both of
them.

After the exciting 3-3 draw, they bumped into
each other outside the dressing rooms.

'Hi, I'm Paul,' Pogba said, offering his hand.

'Don't worry, I know who you are!'

Romelu told Paul the story of the first time he had
heard his name. Paul laughed. 'Fifteen? I knew about
you way before that! I think I was about thirteen.
Everyone knew about Lukaku the beast!'

As they stood there chatting and joking, it felt
like they had been friends for years. They were the

same age, they both spoke French, and they had the same sense of humour. They liked the same things, too – rap music, dancing, basketball and, of course, football.

Romelu took a funny selfie picture to send to his dad and brother. 'They'll be happy to see you again,' he said. 'They're your biggest fans!'

Before the Manchester United coach left Stamford Bridge, Romelu and Paul swapped phone numbers.

'Let's stay in touch!' Paul called out as he waved goodbye.

It was the start of a great football friendship. Every week, they texted or called each other. And whenever Paul was in London, or Romelu was in Manchester, they met up. They went for dinner together, or played video games. It was good to talk because they were in the same difficult position. They were both young, talented and impatient for glory.

'We're not kids anymore – we're good enough to play!'

'At least you've started a game, Rom. I still haven't.'

'One game is nothing, though. I need to play regularly if I'm going to start scoring goals again.'

'Against Blackburn, Sir Alex didn't have anyone to play in central midfield. Scholesy has retired, Darren Fletcher was injured, and Michael Carrick was playing in defence. Surely, he was going to pick me? But no, he picked Rafael instead. A right-back!'

'You should come to Chelsea instead. It would be so cool if we played in the same team together!'

They shared the same big football dreams. 'One day, Rom, one day. But before that, we're going to become superstars. Mark my words – next year is going to be our year!'

But as the 2012–13 season kicked off, Paul was no longer at Manchester United and Romelu was no longer at Chelsea. Paul had moved to Italy to join Juventus, and Romelu was starting a one-year loan at West Bromwich Albion.

'Good luck! Do you even know where West Bromwich is?' Paul joked in a text. 'It's not in London, that's for sure!

'Shut up! At least I'll be starting matches, bro.

You'll be warming the bench and cleaning Andrea Pirlo's boots!'

It wasn't an easy decision for Romelu to leave Chelsea. Didier and Nicolas had both left over the summer, which meant he was probably the club's second-choice striker behind Fernando Torres. Plus, Chelsea had just signed his Belgium teammates Eden Hazard and Kevin De Bruyne.

'Don't go yet – we've just arrived!' they begged.

But Romelu wanted to be first-choice, not second-choice. He wanted regular first-team football and his then-manager at Chelsea, Roberto Di Matteo, couldn't promise that.

'I just need to go away and score some goals,' Romelu told Eden and Kevin. 'But don't worry, I'll be back!'

CHAPTER 16

WEST BROM

'Welcome to West Brom!' manager Steve Clarke said, shaking Romelu's hand. 'As soon as Roberto said that you might be available on loan, I was desperate to get you. This is the perfect place for you to develop.'

Steve had lots of connections at Chelsea. He had spent eleven years at the club as a player and then four more as José Mourinho's assistant.

'It was definitely worth staying in touch!' Steve laughed to himself as he watched the training session.

Romelu had only just arrived at West Brom, but he was starting with a bang. He chased after his opponents like a raging bull, hunting for the ball and for chances to score. The West Brom players were too scared to get close to him. Even their big captain, Jonas Olsson, couldn't tackle him.

'Great finish!' Steve clapped as Romelu scored his second goal of the day.

Romelu was at a new club now and that meant new people to impress, and new competition for places. West Brom had three other attackers – Shane Long, Peter Odemwingie and Marc-Antoine Fortuné – to fill one or two starting spots, and so he was determined to spend as little time on the bench as possible.

In the first Premier League game of the 2012–13 season, he came on for the last twenty-five minutes. West Brom were winning 2–0, and Liverpool were down to ten men. 'A goal on my debut – why not?' he thought to himself as he ran on to the pitch. Romelu was dreaming big.

The West Brom corner was cleared to the edge of the penalty area. Youssouf Mulumbu went for goal but his shot was deflected straight to left-back Liam Ridgewell. In the six-yard box, Romelu moved away from his marker and waited for the cross. His heart was pounding with excitement. When the cross arrived, he remembered his dad's lessons and powered his header past the goalkeeper.

Goooooooooooooooooooooaaaaaaaaaaaaaaaaaaaaaaaall llllllllllllllllllllllllllllllll!!!!!!!!!!!!!!!!

What a start! Romelu raced past the cheering fans behind the goal and celebrated with his new teammates. He felt a wave of joy and relief rush over him. He had finally scored in English football.

'Welcome to West Brom!' Liam cheered in the middle of the big group hug.

Steve was really pleased for Romelu, but he didn't move him straight into the first eleven. 'Right now, you're the perfect super sub. You come on in the second half and cause lots of problems for a tired defence. But I don't think you're ready to play the full ninety minutes yet.'

'YET,' the West Brom manager repeated when he saw Romelu's disappointment. 'Go out there and prove me wrong!'

With Steve's encouragement, Romelu soon forced

his way into the starting line-up. He was West
Brom's only striker against Reading, and their main
goalscoring threat. But after seventy minutes, it was
still 0-0. Romelu looked over at the bench and saw
his manager preparing his substitutions. His time was
running out. All he needed was one chance.

Suddenly, the ball fell to Romelu on the edge of
the penalty area. He had two defenders in front of
him, so he took a touch to control the ball, then
another to shift the ball to the left. When a small gap
opened up, Romelu decided to shoot.

*Goooooooooooooooooooooooaaaaaaaaaaaaaaaaallllllllll
lllllllllllllllllll!!!!!!!!!!!!!!!!!!!!*

Romelu felt on top of the world. Thanks to him,
West Brom won the match and moved up to third in
the table, on the same number of points as Chelsea.

'If you keep scoring like that, they're going to
want you back before the end of the season!' Steve
warned. He really didn't want to lose his star striker.

Romelu shook his head. He was happy to be a
Baggie. 'I'm not going anywhere. I'm improving
here.'

Romelu had a great coach and great teammates too. Every day in training, Jonas gave him a tough time, pushing him around and marking him tightly. It was always an epic battle between them.

'Remember, Premier League defenders will do anything to keep you quiet,' his captain warned him. 'You're a big guy – use that strength of yours!'

Romelu practised holding the ball up and then passing out to the wingers. After that, he turned and ran into the penalty area, looking for the cross or rebound. That was the West Brom game-plan and he had a key part to play.

As the season went on, Romelu got better and better. In January 2013 he scored two goals when he faced Reading for the second time, having scored two against Sunderland. As the end of the season approached, he was West Brom's top scorer with fourteen goals and there was still one huge home game to go: Sir Alex Ferguson's final match in charge of Premier League Champions Manchester United.

'Come on, let's finish on a high!' Jonas told the players in the dressing room before kick-off.

Romelu was on the bench and by half-time, West Brom were losing 3–1. Steve was furious with his team. 'I know that we've already finished eighth, but there's no excuse for that performance. You're not on holiday yet, lads! Rom, you're coming on. Go out there and give the fans something to cheer about.'

Romelu was determined to repay his manager for all of his help and support. He chased after a loose ball and curled a shot straight into the bottom corner.

Goooooooooooooooaaaaaaaaaaaaaaaaaaaallllllllllllllllll llllllllllllllll!!!!!!!!!!!!!!!!!!

3–2! As he ran back for the restart, Romelu gave a big thumbs-up to the supporters, and to Steve.

With ten minutes to go, United were winning 5–2. But as the champions celebrated, Romelu pounced to spoil the party and make a name for himself. With two more goals, he completed his first ever hat-trick, and West Brom finished with a 5–5 draw.

It was almost the perfect way for Romelu to say goodbye. At the final whistle, he felt both happy and sad at the same time. Happy, because he had scored a hat-trick against Manchester United, but sad because

West Brom hadn't won the game, and because his time at the club was over.

'I'll never forget my season here,' he told Steve. 'Thanks, you really changed my life!'

'When I arrived here, I was a kid,' he told Jonas. 'Thanks, you made me a man!'

His captain laughed. 'It's been a pleasure, Rom. Good luck! West Brom vs Chelsea – get ready to carry on our battle next season!'

CHAPTER 17

EVERTON PART I

As he made the long walk from the half-way line to the penalty area, Romelu tried to focus. He tried to ignore the noise of the Bayern Munich fans, the cold stare of their goalkeeper Manuel Neuer, and most of all, the pressure.

That wasn't easy. The 2013 UEFA Super Cup had finished 2–2 after extra-time. Romelu had only been on the pitch for twenty minutes but he was now taking the crucial tenth penalty. If he scored, the shoot-out went to sudden death. If he missed, it was over, and Chelsea would be the losers.

Romelu placed the ball down on the spot and stepped back. 'Keep calm, keep calm,' he repeated to himself. It was definitely the most important penalty of his life. As he waited for the referee's whistle, he stared down at the ball and took long, deep breaths.

Romelu's run-up was short and slow. He was hoping that Neuer would dive early but the German keeper wasn't fooled that easily. He would have to use his power instead. Romelu struck the ball pretty well, but his shot didn't find the bottom corner. Instead, it found Neuer's strong arm.

Saved!

Romelu put his hands on his head and turned away from the goal. He couldn't bear to watch as the Bayern Munich players celebrated their victory. He wanted to be anywhere but in the middle of a big football pitch with thousands of people watching his agony.

'Chin up, mate,' David Luiz told him. 'Taking a penalty in a final takes a lot of courage. Don't forget that.'

'But I missed it!' Romelu replied.

'Don't worry, you'll get plenty of chances to make things right,' David reassured him.

But would he *really*? Four days later, Romelu left Chelsea to spend another season out on loan. If José Mourinho didn't want him in his squad, he'd go and play for someone that did.

*

'Welcome to Everton!' manager Roberto Martínez said, shaking his hand. 'We're so excited to have you here. You're the goalscorer that we've been looking for!'

Romelu was very happy with his new club. He would be playing with talented internationals like Tim Howard, Leighton Baines and Gareth Barry. His new teammates also included a fellow Belgian – Kevin Mirallas – and an old friend.

'We played against each other in a youth tournament about seven years ago – do you remember?' Romelu asked Ross Barkley.

Ross thought for a moment and then his face lit up. 'Yes, I do! No-one could get near you. You scored as many goals as everyone else put together.'

Romelu laughed. 'I've still got the video! I remember thinking that you were going to be a top player. Now we're in the same team!'

With Ross and Kevin supplying the assists from midfield, Romelu hoped to score even more goals than he had at West Brom.

'I'm going to show Mourinho that I can do more than just miss penalties,' he told his family.

Romelu made his league debut as a half-time substitute against West Ham. He was desperate to make a winning, scoring start, just like at West Brom. Leighton scored two amazing free-kicks but with ten minutes to go, Everton still needed a matchwinner.

Romelu was going to be that matchwinner. He believed in himself. As Kevin dribbled forward on the left, he made a late run into the danger zone. Kevin's cross was perfect and Romelu jumped above two West Ham defenders to head the ball down into the bottom corner.

Goooooooooooooooooooooaaaaaaaaaaaaaalllllllllllll lllllllllllllll!!!!!!!!!!!!!!!!

As the Everton fans went wild, Romelu lay on the grass, holding his head. He had clashed with one of the West Ham defenders.

'Rom, you scored!' his teammates told him, but he didn't understand what was going on.

'Rom, you scored!' the physio told him and after some treatment, he finally understood. A smile spread across his face, despite the pain.

'I scored!' he cheered.

By the time the Merseyside derby arrived, Romelu had his shooting boots laced up tight. This was the big game that he had been looking forward to. He could remember watching Everton vs Liverpool games on TV back in Belgium when he was a kid. He couldn't wait to play in such an important match.

'One goal could make you an Everton hero for life!' Ross told him.

Romelu always loved the loud atmosphere at Goodison Park but Derby Day was extra special. The fans had been waiting months for these ninety minutes of football against their bitter rivals.

Despite all of the adrenaline, Everton got off to a terrible start. Liverpool took the lead and were 2–1 up at half-time. Romelu wasn't happy at all. He had barely touched the ball, let alone had a shot on target.

'Come on, we need to test this Liverpool defence,' he told Ross and Kevin. 'It's way too easy for them at the moment. If you put in some crosses and through-balls, I'll score.'

Romelu kept his promise. The ball came to him in the penalty area and he calmly side-footed it into the net.

Goooooooooooooooooooaaaaaaaaaaaaaaaallllllllllllllll llllllllllll!!!!!!!!!!!!!!!

2–2! Romelu slid along the grass on his knees and slapped the corner flag. The fans were on their feet, chanting his name. Romelu stood in front of them and shook his Everton shirt. He was delighted with his goal, but he still had more work to do.

At the corner-kick, Romelu was up against Glen Johnson, who was quite a bit smaller than him. There was only going to be one winner. Romelu leapt high and steered the ball into the top corner. 3–2 to Everton!

Romelu punched the air and roared. He wasn't just

dreaming big anymore; he was scoring big. Thanks to him, Goodison Park was rocking.

'You're definitely an Everton hero now!' Ross shouted joyfully.

Liverpool scored a late equaliser but Romelu was still very proud of his Merseyside derby debut. After the match, he had a text message from his friend Paul Pogba. There were no words, only four flame emojis. Yes, Romelu *was* on fire. *The Guardian* newspaper named him as one of the ten most promising young players in Europe.

'Congrats, but have you seen who's at the top of the list?' Paul teased. 'Me!'

In January 2014, Paul persuaded Romelu to make a bold style change. 'It was time… bye dreads,' he posted on Instagram with a photo of his shaved head.

'Wow, you look so young now!' Paul said when he saw the picture.

As soon as he did it, Romelu started to worry. 'It feels weird. And cold! I had those dreadlocks for years. What if I'm not as good without them? What if they brought me luck?'

Two weeks later, it was time for the second Merseyside derby: Liverpool vs Everton, at Anfield. When Steven Gerrard scored for the Reds, it was double bad news for the Blues. Romelu was down in the penalty area, screaming and clutching his ankle. His own teammate, Gareth Barry, had slipped and crashed into him at the corner.

'Do you think you'll be able to continue?' their goalkeeper Tim Howard asked as he helped Romelu onto his feet.

The Everton physio watched the striker take a few painful steps and shook his head. Romelu's second Merseyside derby was over after only twenty-five minutes. As he left the pitch on a stretcher, he couldn't help thinking about his dreadlocks. Had he made a big mistake?

'How long will I be out for?' Romelu asked the doctor. He was very worried because he had never had a serious injury before.

'Luckily, there's no ligament damage, so it should be weeks, rather than months.'

Romelu's first reaction was relief, but then he

started to think about life without football. What would he do all day? It was going to be awful. And who would score the goals for Everton now?

'Just rest up and then focus on your recovery,' Martínez told him. 'We'll survive for a few weeks, but we need you back!'

Romelu returned in March and finished the season with a bang. He scored against West Ham, Newcastle, Arsenal and Manchester City to finish with fifteen Premier League goals.

'That's only two less than I got at West Brom,' he told Vinnie, 'and I played four less games this season.'

'Eden was Chelsea's top scorer and he only got fourteen,' his friend reminded him. 'Together, you guys could be incredible!'

Yes, it was almost time for Romelu to return to Chelsea and challenge for a starting spot once again. But first, he was off to the 2014 World Cup in Brazil.

CHAPTER 18

BELGIUM

'Everyone's talking about Spain, Brazil, Argentina and Germany, but what about Belgium? It's unlikely, but they *could* win it!'

'Yes, they've got Hazard, Lukaku, Kompany, Fellaini – that's not a bad team, is it? Plus, they're in an easy group!'

Belgium were the big dark horses for the tournament. Romelu was glad to hear people talking about the team, but it put a lot of added pressure on their young, inexperienced squad.

'It's crazy,' he told Eden. 'We didn't even qualify for Euro 2012, but now we're supposed to win World Cup 2014!'

'No, ignore all that talk,' his friend replied. 'We'll just do our best and see what happens.'

Romelu was Belgium's first-choice striker, after scoring three against Luxembourg and one against Sweden in the warm-up matches. Despite the long, tiring Premier League season, he felt ready to shine. He was living his childhood dream, after all.

'It's impossible not to feel excited about playing in a World Cup,' Romelu said to Kevin, as they took in all the colour, noise and movement around them. There was a real party atmosphere in the streets. 'Especially in Brazil!'

Despite his excitement, Romelu struggled in the first two matches against Algeria and Russia. Belgium had lots of possession, but they didn't create many good chances for him. Against Algeria, he didn't have a single touch in the penalty area. Romelu was taken off before the sixty-minute mark in both games, and his team then went on to win without him.

Romelu wasn't happy with the team tactics. He wasn't just a big target man; he was much more talented than that. Why couldn't he be part of the build-up play? He could pass, dribble and create, as well as score. As Romelu left the pitch against Russia, he refused to shake the hand of Belgium's coach, Marc Wilmots, and kicked a boot in frustration. His 2014 World Cup was not going according to plan at all.

Once he had calmed down, Romelu went to apologise to Marc. 'Sorry, I shouldn't have reacted like that. I was just really disappointed.'

'I understand,' the Belgium coach told him. 'I know you're not happy with the way we're playing but I have to do what's right for everyone. If we're going to do well in this tournament, we need you up front, doing what you do best – scoring goals!'

Marc was right. Romelu had to be more of a team player and stop focusing on his own glory. As long as Belgium kept winning, it didn't matter who scored or whose skills were best.

In the Round of 16, they faced the USA, when Romelu would be up against his Everton teammate, Tim Howard.

'I hope you're ready for me to score against you!' Romelu texted him before the match.

'No chance!' Tim replied. 'You're going home without a goal.'

Romelu spent the first ninety minutes on the subs bench, watching as Tim made save after save. He was desperate to get out there and become Belgium's hero. As extra-time started, Romelu finally got his chance.

'Show me what you can do,' Marc Wilmots told him.

This time, Romelu wouldn't let his country down. As soon as he ran onto the pitch, he knew that he was going to score. Everything felt right. When he got the ball on the right, the left-back tried to tackle him, but he was far too strong. Romelu turned and dribbled at full speed towards the penalty area.

He thought about his options. Should he shoot? No, the angle was very tight. Should he pass? Yes, he could see Kevin De Bruyne making a great run. He delivered the cross and Kevin scored. 1–0! Romelu pumped his fists. At last, he had helped his team to score. He ran and joined the happy group hug.

Ten minutes later, Kevin returned the favour.

Romelu burst through the middle of the tired USA defence, calling for the ball. Kevin's pass was perfect; he didn't even need to take a touch. He just smashed the ball past Tim and into the net.

Goooooooooooooooooooaaaaaaaaaaaaaaaaalllllllllllll llllllllllllll!!!!!!!!!!!!!!!!!!

Romelu had scored his first World Cup goal! He ran to the TV camera in the corner and kissed the lens. 'I love you, Papa!' he shouted. It was a moment that he would never forget.

'Yes, Rom, what a finish!' his teammate Daniel Van Buyten screamed in his face. 'We're through to the quarter-finals!'

Despite his match-winning performance, Romelu was still on the bench for the next match against Argentina. He was disappointed, but at least he would get the chance to be a super sub again.

'Don't worry, we're going to come on and make the difference!' he told Dries Mertens confidently. Belgium were losing 1–0.

When Wilmots brought them on, Romelu and Dries had half an hour to save the day. They worked hard to find space, but the Argentina centre-backs were always right behind them. In the final minute, Dries played a brilliant through-ball for Romelu as he ran into the penalty area. The Belgium fans held their breath. Was this the equaliser?

Romelu tried to shoot straight away but the defender blocked him. He still had the ball, though. Romelu looked up and saw Daniel sprinting into the six-yard box. His cross would have to be perfect to reach him. It beat the keeper and rolled towards Daniel... but a defender stretched out his leg to clear it!

Romelu put his hands to his face and looked up at the sky. It just wasn't Belgium's day.

At the final whistle, he stood with his hands on his hips, staring down at the grass. There had been highs and lows, but Romelu's first World Cup was over.

CHAPTER 19

EVERTON PART II

'Do you think you have a future at Chelsea?'

'Have you spoken to Mourinho about next season?'

'Is it true that you don't want to go out on loan again?'

After his World Cup disappointment, Romelu needed a break from football. He wanted to go on holiday with his family and forget about everything for a week, but the media wouldn't let him. They kept asking him the same questions. In the end, Romelu had to reply.

'I want to be somewhere where I can play my best football and hopefully win titles,' he said. 'I've got a decision to make but first, I'm going to relax a little bit!'

When Chelsea bought Diego Costa and re-signed Didier, Romelu's mind was made up. He wasn't going to stay and sit on the bench, and he wasn't going on loan again either. He was twenty-one now and he needed a permanent home. 'Who wants me?' he asked his agent.

Atlético Madrid and Tottenham were interested, but there was a firm offer from his former loan club, Everton. Their manager was determined to sign him.

'Of course we'll get him!' Martínez told the fans.

Romelu had enjoyed his season at Everton. He liked the coaches, the players and the fans. It felt like home. He knew that Martínez really believed in him, and wanted to help him become a truly world-class striker. Everton was a big club, and they needed a star goalscorer. It was the perfect place for Romelu to continue his development.

'I want to go back,' he told his agent.

By the end of July 2014, the deal was done and Romelu was an Everton player again. This time, however, it felt a lot more exciting. At £28million, he was their record signing and he was also the proud new owner of their Number 10 shirt.

'I can't wait to get started again,' Romelu told the reporters. 'I'm looking forward to a successful season.'

But after three games, Romelu hadn't scored any of Everton's seven goals. He had hit the crossbar, but he couldn't get the ball into the net.

'What's wrong with me?' he asked himself.

Romelu reacted to his disappointment with extra finishing practice. After training, he grabbed a big bag of balls and took shot after shot. There was always more work to be done. Sometimes, his manager had to send him home.

'Come on Rom, that's enough for today!' Martínez called out. 'Just be patient. I know you love to be the main man but it's nice to have help sometimes.'

As soon as Romelu relaxed, his chance at scoring a goal finally arrived. A West Brom defender cleared the ball straight to him on the edge of the penalty area. Romelu controlled it and then curled an accurate shot into the bottom corner.

Goooooooooooooooooooooooaaaaaaaaaaaaaalllllllllllll llllllllllll!!!!!!!!!!!!!!

Despite his great joy and relief, Romelu didn't celebrate. He had too much respect for his old club and their fans. He would always have a soft spot for West Brom.

'I'll enjoy it later,' he told his Everton teammates. 'I can watch it again and again on *Match of the Day*!'

The 2014–15 season wasn't Romelu's best in the Premier League but that was partly because Everton were playing lots of matches in other competitions too. Many of his best performances came in Europe. Romelu had loved the Europa League ever since his early days at Anderlecht.

'We could win this tournament!' Romelu told his teammates. He wanted to win more trophies as soon as possible.

After topping their group, Everton took on Swiss team Young Boys in the second round. They weren't a famous club like Real Madrid or Juventus but that didn't mean it would be easy. Romelu was ready for a tough test, especially in the away leg.

'As long as you don't lose, I think that's a decent result,' his dad told him, but he was feeling much more optimistic than that.

'No way, we're going to go there and win, Papa!'

Young Boys took the lead and that made Romelu even more determined. He wasn't scared of anyone, especially not a couple of big centre-backs.

'Cross it!' he shouted.

Gareth delivered a beautiful ball, right on to Romelu's head. There wasn't much pace on the cross, so he went for accuracy, rather than power. The ball bounced past the goalkeeper's outstretched arm and into the bottom corner.

Gooooooooooooooooooooaaaaaaaaaaaaaalllllllllllllllllll llllll!!!!!!!!!!!!!!!!!!!!!

Romelu was delighted. He ran towards the Everton fans and called his teammates over to celebrate with him.

'Great cross,' Romelu told Gareth as they high-fived. 'More of the same please!'

Fifteen minutes later, they did it again. This time, Gareth played a low ball across the goal and Romelu was there at the back post to tap it in.

'Simple, you're the best!' he cheered, giving his teammate a hug.

Romelu was on a hat-trick and it wasn't even half-time yet. All he needed was one more chance. Early in the second half, he ran on to a great long ball. Three defenders chased after him, but they were never going to catch him. As he entered the penalty area, the goalkeeper flew out to block his shot. But Romelu didn't panic. He just lifted the ball over him.

'What a cool finish!' Ross shouted, jumping on the hat-trick hero.

Everton got knocked out in the next round but Romelu still ended up as the joint top scorer in the Europa League with eight goals.

'Well done, twenty for the season is great, bro!' Jordan congratulated him over the summer. 'Isn't that your best total in England?'

'Yes, but I know I can do much better than that,' Romelu replied. 'Ten goals in the Premier League? That's rubbish!'

Romelu was never satisfied. His new target was to

improve his movement in the penalty area. Martínez told him to watch videos of Javier Hernández and Edinson Cavani.

'So, what did you think?' his manager asked him.

Romelu was blown away. 'Those guys are incredible! They're always alert and always thinking. They make it look easy, but it's not. It's really clever. They're like actual hunters!'

Martínez laughed. 'Well, let's turn you into an actual hunter too!'

CHAPTER 20

ROMELU & ROSS

Tim dived low and stretched out his long right arm, but it was no use. He had no chance of saving Romelu's thunder strike. The Everton keeper sighed and picked yet another ball out of his net. 'This isn't fun anymore, Rom,' he said. 'You've always been good, but now you're scary good!'

Romelu couldn't wait for the new season of 2014–15 to start. He felt fit, fired up, and ready to score lots and lots of goals. He had new targets to achieve.

'I'm an experienced Premier League striker now,' he reminded his manager. 'It's time for me to live up to my potential. I'm aiming for thirty goals!'

Martínez laughed. 'I love your ambition. If you

score thirty, I'll be delighted and so will all the fans. But I'll be very happy with twenty-five!'

'Let's see about that!' Romelu replied with a big grin. He had a very good feeling about the season. It was Everton's best team yet.

Against Southampton, Ross dribbled forward on the counter-attack. He passed to Arouna Koné, who crossed to the back post. Romelu jumped and headed the ball past the goalkeeper. 1–0!

Goooooooooooooooooooooaaaaaaaaaaaaaaalllllllllllllll llllllllllllll!!!!!!!!!!!!!!!!

Romelu ran over to Arouna, pointing at his strike partner. As the Everton fans roared, Arouna knelt down and pretended to polish Romelu's boot.

'I scored with my head, you fool!' he joked.

Romelu was playing with so much confidence. He passed to Ross on the half-way line and then sprinted forward for the one-two. Ross' return pass was perfect. Romelu hit a first-time shot. 2–0!

'Easy!' they cheered together.

Romelu's form was the best of his career. He scored against West Brom, Liverpool, Sunderland and

West Ham. Everton's 4–0 win over Aston Villa was 'The Romelu and Ross Show'. Ross scored the first, then Romelu, then Ross, then Romelu again.

'They just can't handle us!' Ross cheered.

Romelu had now scored over fifty Premier League goals and he wasn't even twenty-three yet. 'If I stay in England, I could make it to five hundred!' he told Martínez.

Romelu was only half-joking. He was playing so well that he believed that he could score in every game. By early March, he already had eighteen league goals for the season, his best-ever total. No Everton striker had ever scored so many in one Premiership season. Romelu was very proud of that record. Suddenly, thirty goals didn't look like such a crazy target. He still had three big months of football to go.

In the quarter-finals of the FA Cup, Everton faced his old club Chelsea. Romelu was up against his replacement, Diego Costa. He couldn't wait to prove Mourinho wrong.

'Let's see who has the last laugh!' he texted his friend Paul.

With fifteen minutes to go, Romelu chased after Ross's through-ball. He was on his own, wide on the left, with four Chelsea defenders around him. What could he do?

Romelu never stopped believing. He controlled the ball and then cut inside between the first two defenders. César Azpilicueta tried to stop him but Romelu was far too strong and determined. He was into the penalty area, past another defender, with just one more to beat. The Everton fans were up on their feet, praying for a wondergoal.

Romelu dribbled one way and then the other, leaving Gary Cahill dazed and confused. It was time to shoot. With his left foot, he drilled the ball past the keeper.

Goooooooooooooooooooaaaaaaaaaaaaaaaallllllllllllll llllllll!!!!!!!!!!!!!!!!!!

Goodison Park went wild, but no-one was more excited than Romelu. Not only had he scored against Chelsea, but it was also his best goal ever! As he fell to his knees by the corner flag, his teammates piled on top of him.

'You're a genius!' Ross screamed in his ear.

Romelu wasn't done yet. Five minutes later, he ran on to another Ross through-ball and made it 2–0. This time, he even nutmegged the keeper.

'We're going to Wembley!' Romelu cheered joyfully.

In the end, Everton lost to Manchester United in the FA Cup semi-final, just like they had lost to Manchester City in the League Cup semi-final. It was frustrating to get so close to glory.

'We're good enough to win trophies,' Romelu moaned to Ross. 'We just have to believe in ourselves!'

With no chance of silverware, Romelu's season fizzled out. He didn't score a single goal in his last ten games and Everton finished eleventh in the Premier League. That wasn't good enough and Martínez was sacked.

Romelu was very disappointed to see his manager leave. Martínez had played a very important role in helping him to develop as a striker. 'It wasn't his fault,' Romelu told Ross. 'We were the ones out there playing on the pitch. It was our responsibility.'

When the summer transfer window opened,

Romelu was a wanted man again. There weren't many top strikers in Europe who had scored twenty-five goals that season. Arsenal and Manchester United were looking for a new target man and so were PSG and Juventus. Even Romelu's old club Chelsea were interested.

'If anyone wants to buy Lukaku, they'll have to pay £75 million,' Everton's owner Farhad Moshiri declared. He hoped that the huge price-tag would be enough to put other clubs off. He really didn't want to lose his star man.

'We've got big plans for Everton,' Moshiri explained to Romelu. 'We've got money to spend and we want to build the team around you. You can't leave now!'

Romelu was desperate to win big trophies, but he agreed to give the Romelu and Ross Show one more go at Everton. He loved the club and he wanted to make the fans happy. But if he finished another season empty-handed, he would have to think again about his future.

CHAPTER 21

EURO 2016

Phew! It was a huge relief when Romelu got the call to say that he was in the Belgium squad for Euro 2016.

Despite his great form for his club, he was really struggling to shine for his country. His former Chelsea teammates Eden and Kevin were the heroes who led Belgium to the top of their qualifying group. Romelu only started a few matches and didn't get a single goal.

'You scored against Portugal,' Jordan argued. He was looking forward to playing with his brother at the tournament in France. 'I remember because I set you up!'

'Yes, but that was in a friendly,' Romelu replied. 'It doesn't count. Plus, we lost the game!'

If he wanted to become a star at Euro 2016, Romelu needed to show Marc Wilmots that he was good enough to be Belgium's first-choice striker. The manager had plenty of other options, including Christian Benteke, Dries Mertens and Divock Origi.

Romelu scored in all three of their warm-up matches against Switzerland, Finland and Norway. 'I've done my best,' he told Eden. 'Now I just have to hope that Coach picks me!'

Romelu was delighted to make the starting line-up for Belgium's opening game against Italy. It would be a very tough first test, especially for Romelu against their brilliant defenders Leonardo Bonucci and Giorgio Chiellini. He would have to make the most of any chances that he got.

With Italy winning 1–0, Belgium broke forward on the counter-attack. Kevin played a great pass to Romelu and he was through on goal, with just Gianluigi Buffon to beat. Surely, he was about to make it 1–1! Romelu struck the ball powerfully over Buffon's arms but instead of flying into the top corner, the shot flew over the bar.

Romelu winced. He couldn't believe it. What a chance! He had to be sharper than that. His team needed a goalscorer and he had let them down.

Belgium lost the game 2–0. As he left the pitch, Romelu felt really disappointed with his performance. Italy's defence was very experienced and clever but that was no excuse.

'I'm better than that!' he told himself.

Belgium were one of the favourites to win Euro 2016, but the defeat at the hands of Italy brought them right back down to earth. It was a big setback, but they had to bounce back quickly. 'We absolutely *have* to beat Ireland now,' Romelu told his teammates, but would he even be playing?

'I need you at your best today,' Wilmots told him as he revealed his team. 'Scoring goals – that's your job!'

This was Romelu's last big opportunity to prove himself. Just after half-time, Kevin dribbled forward and passed to him on the edge of the penalty area. It was the Italy game all over again, but could he get it right this time? Romelu took a touch to control the ball and then picked his spot. He went for accuracy over power.

Coooooooooooooooooooooaaaaaaaaaaaaaaaallllllllllllll llllllllll!!!!!!!!!!!!!!

Romelu raced past the Belgium fans celebrating behind the goal. He was proud to make them so happy but he had someone he needed to thank. When he reached Wilmots, he gave his manager a big hug. 'Thanks for believing in me!' he shouted over the noise of the crowd.

'Thanks for scoring!' Wilmots replied with a big smile on his face.

Romelu scored again later on to make it 3–0. Eden played the pass this time and it was an easy finish for Romelu. Wilmots couldn't drop him now! He put a hand to his left ear and listened to the supporters cheering his name.

Lukaku! Lukaku! Lukaku!

Belgium were back on track and the whole squad celebrated together. If they wanted to win Euro 2016, it had to be a team effort.

With another win against Sweden, Belgium would qualify for the second round. They dominated the match, but they were struggling to score the goal that they needed. It just wasn't Romelu's day. A cross went just past his outstretched leg, the goalkeeper made some good saves and the defenders made some good blocks. The one time that Romelu managed to get the ball in the net, the linesman raised his flag. *Offside!*

'No way!' Romelu protested. He had already started celebrating.

With ten minutes to go, Radja Nainggolan finally scored the winner.

'Yes!' Romelu shouted, throwing his arms up in the air. As long as they won, it didn't matter who scored.

Romelu didn't actually score against Hungary in the Round of 16 but he played a big role in Belgium's 4–0 win. Next, the Red Devils were feeling very confident ahead of their quarter-final against Wales. The big teams in the tournament were falling. England and Spain had already been knocked out, and soon either Germany or Italy would be out too.

'Let's do this!' Jordan cheered in the tunnel. He was excited about joining his elder brother in the starting line-up.

Belgium started brilliantly. Romelu set up a golden chance for Yannick Carrasco but the goalkeeper made a great save. Eden and Thomas Meunier took rebound shots but the defenders blocked them both.

'Don't worry, we'll score soon!' Romelu told his teammates. There was no need to panic yet.

He was right. Belgium took an early lead thanks to a wonder-strike from Radja. It was all looking good, until Ashley Williams equalised before half-time.

Romelu looked stunned. 'Who was marking him?' he asked his teammates, but no one seemed to know the answer.

Belgium would just have to score again. Thomas got the ball on the right and curled a beautiful cross into the box. Romelu was unmarked in the middle, standing in between the Welsh centre-backs. All he had to do was get his header on target. He jumped well but the ball skimmed off his forehead and went wide.

'No!' Romelu screamed, staring down at the grass. It was a really bad miss. 'Papa could have scored that in his sleep!' he thought to himself.

A few minutes later, Wales went 2–1 up. It was turning into a disaster for Belgium. They tried and tried but they couldn't fight back. Just after Wilmots took Romelu off, Wales scored again. 3–1!

At the final whistle, the Welsh players cried tears of joy and the Belgian players cried tears of disappointment.

'We should have won that,' Romelu muttered to himself.

First World Cup 2014 and now Euro 2016. Belgium had an amazing group of players, but they kept collapsing in the big matches. Romelu was determined to do better at World Cup 2018.

CHAPTER 22

NEXT LEVEL

Everton's new midfielder Idrissa Gueye dribbled forward and crossed to the back post. Romelu was there, unmarked and eager to score. He wouldn't get a better chance than this. He calmly headed the ball down into the Sunderland net.

Goooooooooooooooooooaaaaaaaaaaaaaaaaaaalllllllllllll llllllllll!!!!!!!!!!!!!!!!!!

Romelu threw his arms up in the air and jogged over to Idrissa. 'Thanks!' he shouted. It was such a relief to finally score. After thirteen matches without a goal, Romelu was back in business.

Just eleven minutes later, he had achieved a hat-trick. As he celebrated, Romelu smiled at the TV camera and held up three fingers, one for each goal. 'I love you, Mama!' he shouted.

Everton's new manager for the 2016–17 season, Ronald Koeman, was delighted. He had worked hard to keep Romelu at the club for another year and now it was paying off. 'This is going to be your season!' he told his star striker.

The Everton team was full of talented players who could help Romelu to score more goals than ever. The full-backs Seamus Coleman and Leighton Baines loved to get forward and put crosses in the box for him. Ross and Kevin were still there in midfield, playing amazing through-balls, and now they had Idrissa and Yannick Bolasie too.

'It's simple,' Romelu often joked. 'You guys do all the hard work and I'll just stand up front and put the ball in the net!'

But it certainly wasn't like that under the new manager. Koeman asked Romelu to chase and press the opposition defenders. 'Don't give them time on the ball. If you charge at them, they're going to make mistakes!'

Romelu needed time to adapt to this new style of football, but he was determined to become an even better player. The best strikers in the world weren't just great goalscorers; they were great all-round footballers. They were strong, quick, clever *and* hard-working.

'That's what I need to be,' Romelu told Vinnie. There was no end to his ambition.

Away at Manchester City in October 2016, Everton were defending well. It was a difficult game for Romelu as the lone striker. All he could do was hold the ball up and try to create a goalscoring opportunity.

Suddenly, one arrived. Yannick flicked the ball on and Romelu chased after it. He was a long way from goal and it was just him against the whole City defence. But he knew that he had the pace and power to go all the way. So did the Everton supporters, who were jumping out of their seats with excitement.

Lukaku! Lukaku! Lukaku!

Romelu dribbled at Gaël Clichy with his right foot

and then, with a drop of the shoulder and a burst of speed, he made space on his stronger left foot. He was going to score; he knew it. The goalkeeper rushed out to block the shot but Romelu slid the ball past him.

Goooooooooooooaaaaaaaaaaaaaaaaaaaalllllllllllllll llll!!!!!!!!!!!!!!!!!!

He had scored another solo wondergoal! Romelu stood in front of the Everton fans in the corner and nodded his head confidently. 'Yes,' he showed them. 'I *am* amazing!'

The supporters sang his name at the tops of their voices:

Rom, Rom, Romelu,

Rom, Rom, Romelu,

Rom, Rom, Romelu,

ROMELU LUKAKU!

The match finished 1–1 but Romelu had proved that he could score big goals in big games. It wasn't true that he only scored against the weaker teams. He was good enough to score against anyone.

But despite Romelu's best efforts, Everton were

still stuck in mid-table. The Toffees were just
too inconsistent. They beat Arsenal but then lost
to Liverpool and drew with Hull. It was a very
frustrating time for Romelu. He scored twice against
Watford, but The Toffees lost 3–2. What more
could he do for the club? He loved Everton, but it
looked more and more likely that it would be his
last season at Goodison Park.

'I want to win trophies!' he admitted to Ross.
Romelu would miss his friend and goalscoring
partner but he had to think about what was best for
his career. 'The Premier League, the FA Cup, the
Champions League. I just don't think I can do that
here. It's time for me to challenge myself against
the best players in the world.'

By Christmas 2016, Romelu was already up
to thirteen league goals, and his form got even
better in 2017. He scored ten goals in nine
games, including four goals in one game against
Bournemouth. He was now the Premier League's
top goalscorer.

'I'm two ahead of Harry Kane!' Romelu told his

dad proudly. After every match, he checked the charts. He was desperate to win the Golden Boot and finish the season with at least one award.

On the very last day of the season, Romelu lost the race against his big striking rival Harry Kane. But twenty-five was still a lot of goals to score in thirty-seven games. He had reached the next level. Romelu was on the shortlists for both the PFA Player of the Year Award and the Young Player of the Year award. He was also named in the PFA Team of the Year alongside Kane.

'What a strikeforce that would be!' they laughed at the awards ceremony in London.

Romelu wouldn't be joining Tottenham but he would be leaving Everton. After a lot of thinking, he had rejected a big new contract. So, where would he go instead? He had a lot of options to choose from. He had proved himself as one of the deadliest strikers in European football. Over the previous five seasons, Romelu had scored sixty-eight Premier League goals. That was more than anyone else except Sergio Agüero.

'First, I'm going on holiday,' he told Vinnie. 'Then, we'll see which team wants me the most!'

Romelu's next move would be the talk of the summer of 2017.

CHAPTER 23

THE MOVE TO MANCHESTER

'Come to United!' Paul begged. 'With me in midfield and you up front, we'll win the league, no problem!'

Romelu was in no rush to decide on his next football club, not while they were on their dream trip to the USA. Romelu and Paul were having so much fun together, relaxing by the pool, driving around in cool cars, playing basketball, and meeting famous rappers. While Paul showed off his new dance moves to his Instagram followers, Romelu watched his friend and laughed.

'Is this why you brought me on holiday?' he teased Paul. 'Is Mourinho paying you to persuade me?'

It was now a two-horse race to sign Romelu – his old club Chelsea versus Mourinho's Manchester United. It was a very difficult decision. Both teams would be challenging for the Premier League and Champions League trophies. At Chelsea he would get to play with Eden, and at United, he would get to play with Paul.

When Vinnie joined them in New York, he asked the crucial question: 'So, who wants you the most?'

'Manchester United,' Romelu replied straight away. It was an easy answer. 'They've offered me three different deals already and Mourinho keeps calling me.'

'What about Chelsea?'

'Antonio Conte has only called me once, and he hasn't even offered me a deal yet. Everything's really slow. It's like they're not sure about me.'

There were rumours in the newspapers that Chelsea wanted to sign Real Madrid's Álvaro Morata instead.

Vinnie shrugged. 'So, what are you waiting for?'

Romelu wasn't exactly sure, but he wanted to take

his time over such an important decision. Wherever he went, he wanted to spend a long time there, perhaps the rest of his career.

When they were out shopping, Romelu's phone buzzed and he picked up. Vinnie tried to listen in but all he could hear was his friend's replies.

'Yes, boss.'

'Okay, boss.'

'Bye, boss.'

'Was that Mourinho?' Vinnie asked and Romelu nodded.

'Wow, he really wants you. And you're calling him "boss" already!'

'I've always called him that, even at Chelsea,' Romelu replied defensively.

Mourinho was the manager who let him go to Everton in the first place. At that time, Romelu was very upset but there were no hard feelings anymore. He had grown up and he was a totally different striker now.

Mourinho called again when they were in LA. 'Have you made a decision yet?' he asked.

'Yes, boss,' Romelu answered, smiling at Paul. 'I'm coming to United!'

Soon, the £75 million deal was done.

'Blessed and delighted to be part of the best football club in the world!' he announced to the world, with a photo of him in a Manchester United shirt.

The only thing left to decide was his number. As the big new striker, Romelu wanted to wear the Number 9 but it still belonged to someone else – Zlatan Ibrahimović.

'I know you might be coming back to United, but can I have the Number 9 shirt this season?' Romelu asked politely on the phone. He didn't want to upset a legend like Zlatan.

'No problem,' he replied. 'When I return, I'll just upgrade to 10!'

In August 2017, Romelu made his Manchester United debut against Real Madrid in the UEFA Super Cup. Four years earlier, he had missed Chelsea's crucial penalty in the tournament, but he forced that thought out of his head. Instead, Romelu focused on scoring goals.

From the very first minute of the match, Romelu made life very difficult for Sergio Ramos and Raphaël Varane. He used his pace to chase every ball and his power to jump for every header. United lost 2–1 but Romelu still scored on his debut. It was a simple tap-in, but he really didn't care about that.

'The boss didn't buy me to score wondergoals,' he told Vinnie. 'He just signed me to score goals – lots of goals!'

There was no stopping Romelu. He scored seven goals in his first seven Premier League matches. He loved playing with Paul and other amazing attacking players like Marcus Rashford, Henrikh Mkhitaryan and Juan Mata. They made life easy for him.

In November 2017, he got off to a flying start in the Champions League too, against FC Basel. As Daley Blind crossed from the left wing, Romelu was being marked by two defenders. They tried to hold him back, but he used his power to jump and head the ball into the net.

Goooooooooooooooooooaaaaaaaaaaaaaaaaaaallllllllllllllll llllll!!!!!!!!!!!!!

Romelu threw his arms out wide and ran towards the corner flag. He felt on top of the world. He had scored his first Champions League goal since his early days at Anderlecht.

'I'm back where I belong!' he shouted out as his teammates hugged him.

Romelu's amazing night ended with some bad news, however. Paul had injured his thigh and would be out for at least a month.

'Sorry, bro,' Romelu told his devastated friend. 'We're going to miss you in midfield but don't worry. We'll keep winning without you!'

At first, they did. Manchester United won their next four matches but there were tougher challenges ahead.

As a former Everton star, Romelu couldn't wait to play against Liverpool. He had scored goals in the Merseyside derby and now he had the chance to score goals in English football's biggest rivalry. With one matchwinner, Romelu could become Manchester United's new hero.

'This is our first big test of the season,' Mourinho

told his players in the dressing room. 'If we want to keep up with City at the top of the league, we can't lose this!'

United didn't lose but they also didn't win. It was a very frustrating afternoon for Romelu because he played up front on his own. It was like the 2014 World Cup all over again. His teammates defended well but they weren't getting forward to support him in attack. For the first thirty minutes, he barely touched the ball. In the end, Romelu went looking for it. Out on the right, he beat the defender and dribbled down the wing, but his cross was too high.

'Rom, we need you in the box on the end of those crosses!' Mourinho shouted, pointing to the middle. 'Let Henrikh and Anthony create chances for *you*!'

Just before half-time, Romelu picked up Henrikh's clever pass and burst into the box. This was the chance he'd been waiting for, his chance for glory. He struck his shot powerfully, but it was too close to Simon Mignolet, who made the save.

Romelu put his hands on his head. 'I should have scored that!' he told himself angrily.

It turned out to be Romelu's only real chance of the match. At the final whistle, he trudged off the pitch, replaying that shot in his head. What a missed opportunity!

'I think he was just trying too hard to score the big goal today,' Thierry Henry said on TV. The former Arsenal striker was now one of Romelu's coaches with the Belgium national team.

'Don't worry about it,' Mourinho told his disappointed striker in the dressing room. 'You missed that one, but you'll score the next!'

But Romelu didn't score against Huddersfield Town, or Benfica, or Tottenham. Despite his great start at Manchester United, the fans weren't happy.

'He's lazy – he needs to work harder for the team!'

'It's one thing scoring against West Ham and Swansea, but Lukaku's not good enough to score against the top teams.'

On his big return to Stamford Bridge, Romelu just couldn't get going. His confidence had completely disappeared. To make matters worse, Álvaro Morata scored Chelsea's winning goal.

'Mama, maybe they were right to sign him instead of me,' Romelu admitted sadly on the phone. It was one of the lowest moments of his career so far. Zlatan Ibrahimović would be back from injury soon. Would he take Romelu's place?

'Son, it's no good feeling sorry for yourself,' Adolphine replied sternly. 'You've got to put all that behind you and come back fighting. Do you remember all the criticism you got when you were younger?'

'Yes, Mama.'

'The other parents said that you were cheating, that you weren't the right age. Then when I showed them your passport, they said you were only good at football because of your size. But you didn't just give up, did you?'

'No, Mama.'

'No, you carried on and proved them wrong. So, pick yourself up and do it again!'

Romelu's comeback started with three goals for Belgium, including a very special goal against Japan in November 2017. With a simple header at the back post, Romelu became his country's record goalscorer at the age of twenty-four.

'Congratulations!' Roberto Martínez said after the game, giving him a big hug. Romelu's former manager at Everton was now his manager at Belgium. 'You're back!'

Yes, Romelu was starting to feel like his old, goalscoring self again. It was time to show Manchester United how good he could be. And his friend was back to help him.

'Did you miss me?' Paul asked, doing a silly dance across the dressing room.

Newcastle took the lead, but they couldn't spoil Romelu and Paul's big day. Paul set up United's first goal and scored the third.

'Right, you need to get one now!' he told his friend as they celebrated.

Romelu was determined to score. He dribbled in from the right wing and played a lovely one-two with Juan. He was into the penalty area, with only the goalkeeper to beat. Romelu faked to shoot and as the goalkeeper dived, he smashed the ball into the top of the net.

Goooooooooooooooooaaaaaaaaaaaaaaalllllllllllllllllllll llllllll!!!!!!!!!!!!!!

The fans cheered, but Romelu didn't even smile. He just stood still, spread his arms and nodded. 'Yes,' he showed them. 'I *am* amazing!'

Romelu's journey from Wintam to Manchester United hadn't always been easy. There had been setbacks and disappointments along the way, but no matter what people said, his talent and belief always shone through. With Paul by his side, Romelu was ready to conquer the world. He was ready to win the biggest trophies and become the best striker around.

Turn the page for a sneak preview of
another brilliant football story by
Matt and Tom Oldfield. . .

POGBA

Available now!

CHAPTER 1

POGBACK

'This is a must-win match,' José Mourinho told his Manchester United team before their home game against Premier League champions Leicester City. 'Today, we need our leaders to lead.'

Paul knew that he was one of the leaders that Mourinho was talking about. His £89 million return to Old Trafford had been the biggest transfer story of summer 2016. The '#PogBack' campaign had taken over the Twittersphere and thousands of fans bought his '6 POGBA' shirt and copied his cool tricks and hairstyles.

After moving to play for Juventus at the age of eighteen, four years later Paul was back at Manchester

United. The French player had established himself as an international superstar and a four-time Italian league winner. Expectations were very high. Ever since Paul Scholes's retirement, United had been seeking a match-winning midfielder and Paul fitted the bill: a box-to-box midfielder who could tackle, dribble and shoot. He was part-Patrick Vieira, part-Zinedine Zidane and part-Ronaldinho, and he would bring glory days back to Old Trafford. That was Mourinho's big plan when he took over as manager.

But after a great start to the new season against Southampton, United had lost two matches in a row to local rivals Manchester City and then to Watford. Lots of people were already criticising Paul. Was he really as good as people said he was? Why wasn't he controlling games? Why hadn't he scored any goals? Why had United paid so much money for him?

'Don't listen to the negative comments,' his mum, Yeo, told him. She was a very important part of Paul's life, offering advice and support when he needed it most. 'We all know how good you are!'

English football was much faster and more physical

than Italian football. Paul needed time to adapt, to gel with his new teammates and to rediscover his form. But he didn't have time. The Manchester United fans were impatient for success.

'We've spent lots of money on great new players,' they argued. 'We have to win the league this season!'

'It's time to shine,' Paul said to himself as he walked out of the tunnel and onto to the Old Trafford pitch. The noise of the crowd only added to his adrenaline. With 70,000 fans cheering his name, it really was the Theatre of Dreams. Paul was a cool character and he never felt nervous, even when the pressure was on. He believed in his own talent and he was determined to win. Today, his usual dyed blond hair was gone; Paul meant business.

From the kick-off, he pushed the team forward with his quick passing and powerful runs. United took the lead through a Chris Smalling header and it gave them the confidence to keep attacking. Leicester just could not cope with the pace and trickery of Jesse Lingard, Marcus Rashford, and especially Paul. He was running the show.

As he dribbled forward, he chipped an amazing pass through to Zlatan Ibrahimović, who chested the ball down and volleyed just over the bar.

'That would have been the best goal ever!' Paul said with a big smile on his face. He was really enjoying himself.

When Paul got the ball on the left, he only had one thought: shoot. He cut inside and hit a rocket of a shot. *Boooooooooom!* The ball swerved through the air. The goalkeeper had no chance but it struck the post.

'Nearly!' Paul said to himself. 'Next time, I'll score.'

Juan Mata dribbled forward and passed to Paul. Without taking a touch to control the ball, he flicked a beautiful pass to Jesse, who flicked the ball into Juan's path. Juan fired into the net to complete a great team goal.

'What an unbelievable move!' Marcus shouted as they all celebrated together.

United's team were on fire and three minutes later, Marcus made it 3–0. Then just before half-time, Daley Blind swung a corner into the penalty area.

Paul used his strength and height to get past his marker and head the ball into the far corner.

Goooooooooooooooooooaaaaaaaaaaaaaaaaaaaaaa llllllllllllllllllllllllllllllllll!!!!!!

Paul finally had his first Manchester United goal and it was an amazing feeling. The supporters expected to see his trademark celebration, 'The Dab', but they would be disappointed. Instead, Paul pointed towards the sky and breathed a sigh of relief. He was finally off the mark, four years after making his club debut, and he was starting to prove his critics wrong.

'Congratulations, that will be the first of many!' Jesse said, giving his friend a big hug.

It was the kind of man-of-the-match performance that Mourinho had broken the world transfer record for. Each time Paul got the ball, every touch was positive and exciting, and the Manchester United fans cheered loudly and hoped for another goal. He was the heart of the team, just as Mourinho had told him to be.

'That's much better!' the manager told him at the

final whistle. 'You're a world-class player and you showed that today.'

Paul was pleased with his display and, most importantly, with the three points from the win. He had returned to Old Trafford dreaming of winning the biggest trophies: the Premier League, the FA Cup and the Champions League. Every victory was a step towards achieving those goals.

'Yes, but I can do even better,' Paul replied, full of confidence.

He was always looking to improve. He had learnt from the best – Patrick Vieira, Zinedine Zidane, Paul Scholes and Andrea Pirlo – and he was still learning from the best. Superstars like Zlatan and Wayne Rooney had lots of experience and tips to share. Paul was ready to do everything possible to be the best midfielder in the world.

He had come a long way from the Renardière estate in France but he was still the same Paul he had always been. He was curious, competitive, gifted, unique, but above all, a born leader and a born winner.

ROMELU LUKAKU HONOURS

Anderlecht
🏆 Belgian Pro League: 2009–10

Chelsea
🏆 FA Cup: 2011–12

Individual
🏆 Belgian Pro League top scorer: 2009–10
🏆 UEFA Europa League Top Goalscorer: 2014–15
🏆 Premier League PFA Team of the Year: 2016–17

LUKAKU

9

THE FACTS

NAME: ROMELU
MENAMA LUKAKU
BOLINGOLI

DATE OF BIRTH:
13 May 1993

AGE: 24

PLACE OF BIRTH:
Antwerp

NATIONALITY: Belgium

BEST FRIEND: Paul Pogba

CURRENT CLUB: Manchester United

POSITION: ST

THE STATS

Height (cm):	190
Club appearances:	337
Club goals:	157
Club trophies:	2
International appearances:	65
International goals:	31
International trophies:	0
Ballon d'Ors:	0

★ ★ ★ **HERO RATING: 86** ★ ★ ★

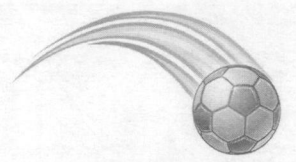

GREATEST MOMENTS

Type and search the web links to see the magic for yourself!

1 **22 AUGUST 2009,**
ZULTE WAREGEM 0–2 ANDERLECHT

https://www.youtube.com/watch?v=0lH52UYXYUA
Romelu didn't score on his first-team debut but he didn't have long to wait. He was still only sixteen when he stretched out his long leg to tap in Mbark Boussoufa's cross. It wasn't Romelu's greatest ever goal, but it was his first. Once Anderlecht's rising star was off the mark, there was no stopping him.

1 JULY 2014,
BELGIUM 2–1 USA

https://www.youtube.com/watch?v=r51_9J2Y9-c
Romelu started the 2014 World Cup as Belgium's first-choice striker, but he soon lost his place to Divock Origi. Romelu didn't give up, however. He came off the bench in the Round of 16 to save the day for his country. After setting up Kevin De Bruyne's first goal, he then scored the matchwinner with a brilliant first-time strike.

12 MARCH 2016,
EVERTON 2–0 CHELSEA

https://www.youtube.com watch?v=4DGjJTvfZR8&t=223s
In the FA Cup quarter-final, Everton were up against the club that had let Romelu go. He had a big point to prove and, boy, did he prove it! Romelu dribbled through the entire Chelsea defence on his own to score an absolute wondergoal. He then made it 2–0 by nutmegging the keeper! Revenge was sweet.

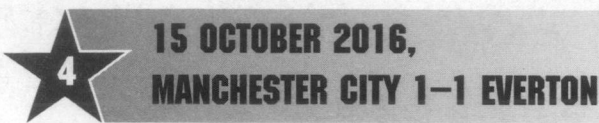

4   15 OCTOBER 2016, MANCHESTER CITY 1–1 EVERTON

https://www.youtube.com/watch?v=2WMfpl7H9uI&t=111s

'He's good but can he score in the big games?' the critics asked. Romelu answered with a fantastic solo strike away at City. His run started in his own half and ended with him dribbling past Gaël Clichy to give Everton the lead. The goal was a clear sign that Romelu had reached the next level.

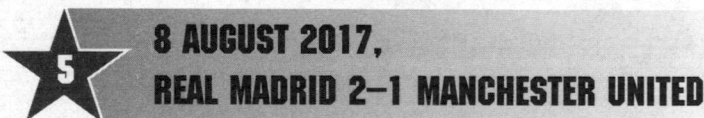

5   8 AUGUST 2017, REAL MADRID 2–1 MANCHESTER UNITED

https://www.youtube.com/watch?v=MfHjXmlGJ5s

Romelu didn't win the UEFA Super Cup on his Manchester United debut, but he did get off to a goalscoring start. With the pressure on, he beat Sergio Ramos to the rebound and calmly shot into the bottom corner. What a moment! United's new £75 million striker was off the mark against the European Champions.

PLAY LIKE YOUR HEROES

THE ROMELU LUKAKU HEADER

SEE IT HERE YouTube

https://www.youtube.com watch?v=EAWRV0GThIs&t=314s

STEP 1: Make sure you're in the middle of the penalty area. If you're not in the danger zone, you can't score!

STEP 2: As the ball is crossed into the box, move towards it, watching it carefully.

STEP 3: Before you jump for the header, use your amazing strength to outmuscle your marker. You want as much space as possible.

STEP 4: Once you're in the right position, leap into the air and hang for as long as you can.

STEP 5: As the ball floats towards your head, use your incredible neck muscles to flick it powerfully towards the goal.

STEP 6: Aim low! Make sure you get over the ball, heading it down into the bottom corner. The keeper isn't saving that.

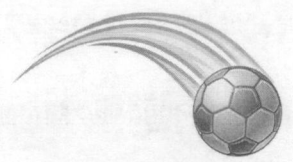

TEST YOUR KNOWLEDGE

QUESTIONS

1. Who first taught Romelu and Vinnie how to head the ball?

2. Who was Romelu's other football hero when he was growing up?

3. Why did Romelu have to move from Rupel Boom to KFC Wintam when he was ten?

4. What was the name of the academy programme that Anderlecht set up for Romelu?

5. How old was Romelu when he made his Anderlecht first team debut?

6. How many goals did Romelu score for Chelsea?

7. Which Chelsea manager allowed Romelu to join Everton permanently?

8. Which striker outscored Romelu to win the 2016–17 Premier League Golden Boot?

9. Who did Romelu make his Manchester United debut against, and did he score?

10. How many goals has Romelu scored for Belgium in big international tournaments?

11. Can you name three shirt numbers that Romelu has worn during his club career?

Answers below. . . No cheating!

1. Romelu's dad, Roger. **2.** Chelsea striker, Didier Drogba. **3.** The family car broke down and they couldn't afford to get a new one. **4.** Purple Talents **5.** 166. **07.** José Mourinho. **8.** Harry Kane. **9.** It was against Real Madrid and yes, he scored on his debut! **10.** 3 (1 at the 2014 World Cup and 2 at Euro 2016.) **11.** Any of 9, 10, 14, 17, 18, 20 and 30.

HAVE YOU GOT THEM ALL?

FOOTBALL HEROES

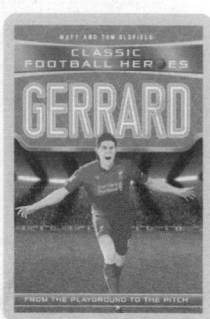